Books by James Thomas Flexner

States
Dyckman

States Dyckman. Artist Unknown.
Courtesy Boscobel Restoration, Inc.

States
Dyckman

American Loyalist

James Thomas Flexner

FORDHAM UNIVERSITY PRESS
New York
1992

Library of Congress Cataloging-in-Publication Data
Flexner, James Thomas, 1908–
States Dyckman : American loyalist / James Thomas Flexner.—1st pbk. ed.
p.   cm.
Originally published: Boston : Little, Brown, 1980.
Includes bibliographical references and index.
ISBN 0-8232-1369-2 (pbk.)
1. Dyckman, States Morris. 2. American loyalists—Biography.
I. Title.
[E278.D97F55   1992]
973.3'14'092—dc20
[B]   92-8063
CIP

Contents

List of Illustrations

States Dyckman

American Loyalist

Prologue

BIOGRAPHERS, almost without exception, limit their concern to individuals who played in their environments a determining part. The witnesses to history; the participants who turn wheels they do not control; multitudes who obey rather than command: these are usually visible only as shadowy figures dimly illuminated by spotlights focused above them; as presumably simple subjects suited to academic beginners; as anonymous units in broad generalizations; or, even more ignominiously, as numerals in sociologists' tables. Thus, the historical process is warped, important sources of human testimony slighted.

The fact that professionally written biographies deal almost exclusively with persons of note forces a deprivation more serious even than the narrowing of historical testimony. The majority of humanity is excluded from the biographer's art.

Common men, even if like States Dyckman they walk uncommon paths, follow different patterns of behavior from people who become great or destroy themselves, sometimes committing murder, in an effort to become so. The difference was brought home to me increasingly by contrasts between Dyckman's behavior and that of the major figures of whom I had written. The break stems from opposite attitudes of the individual towards his environment. Persons who become outstanding are driven by what seems an innate need to shape their worlds, whether seen

[3]

from an artist's studio or a national capital, into patterns of their own devising. Persons like Dyckman float on currents they do not attempt to stem or control, trying, as they are swept along, to maneuver around reefs that automatically appear before them, to edge into eddies that will carry them in what available directions they prefer.

His private life is much more important to a common man than to a leader: in essence, it is all that he has. He cannot find exterior escape from mental agonies or bury domestic tragedy under the grandeur of state or the glories of art. If, like States Dyckman, he does not find solace in theoretical conceptions, religious or otherwise, he is forever dominated by the events of the moment. Unexalted people seem much more imprisoned in their own flesh than persons who shake continents. The fall of the mighty is lighted by setting suns, but the fall of a sparrow testifies to the tragedy of all creation.

It is partly because of an established fashion among readers that biographies of persons not well known are so rarely written. I undertook this life of States Dyckman against a chorus of warnings that only a thin scattering of readers would broach an historical account of a man never previously mentioned in history books. When I pointed out that novelists used as titles of successful works the names of imaginary characters, of course previously unknown, the reply came that those were novels: who would take the trouble to see whether they were interested in a man who actually lived called States Morris Dyckman?

I will confess that this opposition only made me the more determined. I have just spent years writing about the greatest of the American great. Was I to be frightened away from trying an experiment at a different extremity of the biographer's art?

A professional biographer, at liberty after completing his current manuscript, surveys the historical scene for a new protagonist who will keep him interested during a long period of daily association, and who sheds a fascination that the writer believes he can communicate to the reader. His exploring eye is naturally drawn to the well-known, where importance is manifest and documentation clusters. There has to be something of a fluke in the discovery of an engrossing subject still obscured in shadows, concerning whom adequate documentation has by good fortune been preserved.

I would never have happened on States Dyckman had he not sought, when he was dying, to drown the tribulations of his life in the glory of erecting a resplendent mansion. The house, which he called Boscobel, went through its own tribulations, being once sold to a wrecker for thirty-five dollars and rescued by neighbors who lay down before the bulldozers. Eventually, Boscobel re-emerged as a public museum. In the process of restoration, the States Dyckman Papers were exhumed. They were called to my attention and I became moved by his tribulations and excited by his career.

I was particularly intrigued because Dyckman was such a figure as realistic novelists construct from their observations as they walk ordinary paths. He might have been a neighbor whom you often see at the country store or the post office before discovering that he had had strange and enthralling experiences which explain the nervous tugging of his face.

I have in various books been concerned with ways for bringing to biography such virtues of the novel as can be assimilated without violating the biographer's duty to present truthfully what actually took place. This entails starting at an opposite point from a novelist who, having selected an historical protagonist, makes use of what historical fact can be made to suit his imaginative ends. Both literary directions have validity — but only if pursued honestly. To claim to be simultaneously a novelist and a biographer (as some novelists do to the great swelling of their pocketbooks) is patent dishonesty. Indeed, as each is faithful to his own needs, the biographer and the novelist can find no legitimate meeting place. Each, as he tries to add to his armory some weapons more characteristic of the other, only cheapens himself if he deserts the fundamentals of his own craft. This book on States Dyckman has been as conscientiously studied as the driest Ph.D. thesis.

Born in 1754 or 1755, on farmland on Manhattan Island, Dyckman was of the American Revolutionary generation. He inhabited places and times through which I have, as a writer, traveled again and again in pursuit of more exalted individuals: medical scientists, painters, inventors, a traitor and a spy, George Washington and Alexander Hamilton. It soon became manifest to me that Dyckman's adventures elucidated important forces which played, almost unnoticed by historians, a major role in inciting the American Revolution and determining its outcome.

The broad historical category into which Dyckman falls has, it is true, recently, after two centuries of neglect, become a subject for concentrated research: Dyckman was one of that large minority of Americans who remained loyal to the crown and were driven by the Revolution into exile, temporary or permanent. But, unlike the Loyalists who are now attracting attention, he was not a well-born upholder of old standards, who supported and went under with a society greatly to his advantage. Dyckman was one of those Loyalists who seem inexplicable: men from unimportant families with little property, who, although unmoved by strong political convictions, accepted persecution and exile.

After being, as a young man, arrested and temporarily imprisoned, Dyckman sneaked through the military lines from patriot territory to British-occupied New York City. He became a clerk in the Quartermaster Department of the British army. His superiors were siphoning into their own pockets what would be, in modern currency, hundreds of millions of dollars: more than three quarters of the sums paid out by the Crown to buy land transport for the largest expeditionary force mounted by any European power during the eighteenth century. Having played his assigned role in the surreptitious collection of profits, Dyckman accompanied an employer to London where he became, although inconspicuously, a major operator in protecting his exalted and highly visible superiors from investigations mounted by Parliament and the Lords of the Treasury.

Had Dyckman been concerned with a simple case of theft and the protection of the malefactors, the historical importance of his activities would have been small, nor would the investigations have dragged on for twenty-four years to be halted at last by the personal intervention of a Royal Duke, the King's brother. No conclusion had previously been reached because no prosecutor had ever wished to push too hard. Basically, even if the circumstances were extreme, a fundamental and necessary aspect of the British aristocratic way of life had been on trial. This aspect contributed both to the outburst of the American Revolution and to the eventual outcome. The way English tax money tended to end up in private pockets had been a reason why informed men like Franklin opposed English taxation in America; and the vast expense of continuing the war was among the strongest arguments brought forth in Parliament for accepting the independence of the United States. The Dyckman Papers present a startling picture of the pervasive prerogative and corruption in British high places that did so much to make the victory of the less sophisticated Americans possible.

Dyckman received, in return for his services, more than three million modern dollars. But as an American Loyalist, whose father had been a radical, he had, in relationship with his condescending British clients, his pride very carefully to keep. We shall see the expedients by which this able, shy, proud, sickly, and sensitive American tried to make his peace with the hierarchical British world. He turned to personal extravagance and the exercise of taste. Eventually, long after the Revolution was over, the former Loyalist adopted in rage many of the attitudes of the revolutionaries he had to his peril once refused to join. From his lodgings in London, he wrote angrily that he would not be condescended to by his highborn clients. They were not his patrons, as they assumed; he was *their* patron since he enabled them to keep and enjoy the vast fortunes they had pocketed. Dyckman could not menace leaders of British society, as the Continental Congress had done, with the firepower of muskets, but he had in his possession incriminating papers. His threats to make these public were given double power because his intimate friend and coadjutor was the fiery polemicist William Cobbett.

Although he seems to have sired an illegitimate son (whom his wife later sheltered), Dyckman remained a bachelor until middle age. The major emotion of his young manhood was his love for a much younger sister which contributed to her making a disastrous marriage. When Dyckman came home to the Hudson Valley from his first London stay, he discovered that his sister had become addicted to laudanum. Fighting all the while with her truly monstrous husband, he faithfully and painfully brought her back to health. Then he himself married, over the opposition of his bride's family, a better born and much younger beauty. At about the same time, his obsessive extravagance joined with the dishonesty of one of his English "patrons" to drive him to the verge of bankruptcy. He reacted with rage and humiliation that carried him back to England and dangerously close to madness.

CHAPTER ONE

∽

Genesis of a Loyalist

THE spotlight of historical record first struck directly on States Morris Dyckman when at Cartright's Inn at Albany, New York, he raised his glass to drink a toast. The occasion was a celebration of George III's birthday; the date, June 4, 1776; the celebrants, the conservative leaders and royal officials of New York's second city. Dyckman was twenty-two years old. The toast: "Damnation to the enemies of the King."

This was exactly a month before the Continental Congress voted the Declaration of Independence. As the dinner proceeded, the hilarity of the drinkers was interrupted by a distant sound of shouting. Rapidly the shouting approached, becoming ever more distinctly a howl of angry voices, and then there poured into Cartright's Inn a mob of Sons of Liberty. They seized the celebrants. Dyckman was with the others taken before the Committee of Correspondence and jailed.

When the yeoman's son refused to recant by signing an "association" drawn up by the Congress, he became an outlaw from the American Revolution. His freedom and his property, if not his life, were endangered.

Concerning Dyckman's background and childhood, the historical documents reveal much that is explanatory of his character and career.

Jan Dyckman, an immigrant from Westphalia who arrived in 1662, established the family on the northern tip of Manhattan Island. He became a farmer and orchardist, as his son Jacob was after him. Although Manhattan's northernmost east-west thoroughfare is called Dyckman Street, the family were yeoman almost indistinguishable from their farmer neighbors.

The terrain where States grew up is now deeply buried in New York City, but was then buried deep in the countryside. The eighteenth-century city occupied only some three miles of the opposite extremity of the long and narrow island.

For a Dyckman to traverse by farmer's cart the intervening ten miles or so of rough road would take at least two hours, the time it takes a modern automobile to go more than a hundred miles. States's childhood domain was, indeed, a community apart. Separated off from the rest of the world, the inhabitants married each other: States's childhood was lived among cousins.

The father of the future Loyalist, Jacob Dyckman, Jr., was not satisfied with the quiet ancestral life of plow and orchard and crop. He wished to be in the center of things, associating with people of importance, and the best way in colonial times for a man who was not a gentleman to achieve these ends was to become a tavern keeper. Jacob sold his other property to gain possession of a geographical conformation that modern New Yorkers, who think they know their city, cannot believe actually existed.

Meandering between modern 106th and 110th streets, Harlem Creek flowed into the East River, at its largest some hundred feet wide and fifty deep. It was surrounded by an impassable marsh which extended irregularly on and from the riverbank between 91st and 144th streets. Nothing of this is visible today in the packed city except the little pond at the northeast of Central Park known as the Harlem Meer.

Beyond the present Fifth Avenue this complete block to through travel changed from water and marshland to rocks.

Cliffs, rising to more than a hundred feet, extended almost across the entire rest of the island. Near the middle, there was a gap about two hundred feet wide. What came to be known as McGown's Pass was considered so strategic that it was fortified during the Revolution and the War of 1812.

Manhattan was surrounded by waters too considerable for the eighteenth century to bridge except at the northern end where a single bridge, spanning the Harlem River, gave access to the mainland. Only two roads ran the whole length of the island to connect the bridge with the city. Bloomingdale Road (now Broadway) slipped beyond the central barrier along the Hudson shore. The more traveled Post Road moved through McGown's Pass. Here States's father built "a commodious brick house" before which he hung a sign on which was painted a black horse. There were three rooms on a floor with a fireplace in each, "a good cellar and a milk house." The nine acres of land did not permit much farming but in among the rocks Dyckman put a "young bearing orchard of 120 grafted apple trees, pears, etc." It was in the Black Horse Tavern that States Dyckman was born in 1754 or 1755.

His father did not visualize the tavern as a mere wayside accommodation. (There were so many of these along the Post Road that no traveler needed to remain thirsty for more than a mile or so.) The Black Horse had indeed been briefly, during a smallpox epidemic in 1752, capital of the Colony of New York, the Assembly convening "in ye new room." The Black Horse was also a rendezvous for sportsmen. The area was considered excellent for fox hunting.

New York was the most aristocratic of the colonies in America, even more so than Virginia, because so much of the best accessible land was owned by a few great families that were interrelated by marriage. The innkeeper got to know the younger, more sportive patricians. He felt acutely, as his son was to do, the value for men of simple birth to secure the countenance of the great. Jacob got up the courage to ask Staats Morris, member of a family that owned much of the present Borough of the Bronx, whether he might not name his newborn son Staats Morris Dyckman. When the patrician agreed, the father felt he had established for his son a valuable and permanent legacy: a rich well of patronage.

In March, 1756, Jacob Dyckman advertised his tavern for sale. Staats Dyckman was only one or two. However, if we accept the contention that infants are marked by events which took place before the dawn of conscious memory, his family's unhappiness about the situation may have given its first impetus to what was to be a salient aspect of his career. That the advertisement recommended the property as "a gentleman's seat" not a business opportunity indicated that the father had failed to make the tavern pay. The family had been slipping into a humiliating defeat. From the total story of Jacob's life, we may deduce the trouble: States's father was devoted to expensive gestures and expansive schemes.

Jacob's sister-in-law, Catherine Benson McGown, decided that with good management the tavern could be made to pay. (She was to do so well that McGown's Pass was named after her successful hostelry.) Her sea-captain husband had vanished into the ocean and she needed for herself and her children a means of livelihood. Dyckman's advertisement had promised that he could give "a good title" to the property. He hid from the widow as she bought an encumbering mortgage.

Jacob soon was all enthusiasm about what he considered a more propitious place for a tavern. He would set up, on the ancestral property, the inn that would be the closest of all to the crucial bridge across the Harlem River.

However, King's Bridge belonged to Colonel Frederick Philipse, who also owned the best land beyond the bridge all the way up to the Croton River. Philipse made his monopoly expensive, inconvenient, and sometimes impossible to cross. When a penny was a substantial sum of money, he charged as toll ninepence for a carriage, threepence for each riding horse or head of cattle, one penny for a pedestrian. The gates were barred at night. Even in the worst weather, belated travelers had to knock it seemed interminably in the hope of rousing a servant who lived several hundred feet away on the Manhattan side.

Philipse's block to free movement was an economic liability to the whole community, particularly Dyckman's new tavern. It clogged the feet and sandpapered the emotions of those who lived at the top of the island. Perhaps at the tavern, certainly with Dyckman's leadership, the local farmers decided to revolt against the tyranny of the patroon. The inhabitants would erect their own bridge from Dyckman's land to a part of the mainland not controlled by Philipse. Furthermore, stepping towards what would today be called popularism or socialism, they repudiated the system of tolls by which the community leaders profited from the improvements they built and owned. Paid for by popular subscription, the bridge would be free for all comers. Years later, the *New York Gazette* stated that the bridge had been "the first step towards freedom in this state."

To moderns used to crossing the Harlem River on tall, long, and elaborate bridges, the project of the local farmers and carpenters has a ridiculous sound. But the unimproved Harlem River was then narrower and shallow; there was no need to keep navigation open to more than rowboats. The greatest impediment was the enraged Philipse. He used his official position to draft into the militia twice in one year Benjamin Palmer, who was superintending the erection of what came to be known as Palmer's, Dyckman's, or more commonly the Free or the Farmer's Bridge.

The workmen, like the entrepreneurs, were mostly States's relations. The child watched piles driven with sledgehammers to the bottom of the river, while men with shovels and hoes piled up and graded ramps. Then the wooden floor was put across: eighteen feet wide between railings.

Finally, there came what could not help being a banner day in States's childhood. On January 1, 1759, the *New York Gazette* ran the following notice: "These are to acquaint the public that to-morrow . . . the FREE BRIDGE erected and built across the Harlem River will be finished and completed. All gentlemen and ladies of this Province and also in Connecticut and the adjoining Provinces, that have their king and country's good, freedom, and prosperity at heart, are desired to repair to said free bridge . . . where they may see the same finished completely; and which unites this City of New York and the country with a free passage . . . and no tollage, locks, or bars to hinder. On the same day there will be a stately ox roasted whole as a small entertainment to the loyal people who come."* The notice ended with asking those who had not paid up their subscriptions to send the money in.

Although this was fifteen years before the Revolution (which was so to change States's life), the bridge builders felt it necessary to make clear that their action was not in opposition to the British Crown: only "loyal people" were invited to the barbecue. The farmers who were rebelling against the monopoly of a great landholder and by extension against aristocratic privilege had the effrontery to describe their act as serving "the king's and country's good, freedom, and prosperity."

It must have been a great party as the huge carcass of an ox

---

*Except where otherwise indicated, I have modernized in all quotations the spelling and punctuation. Although I realize that this is contrary to scholarly practice, I believe it enables the modern reader to interpret more accurately what is quoted. Dwelling on the variances of eighteenth-century orthography casts a "Ye Olde Gifte Shoppe" quaintness over straightforward prose. Erratic spelling and punctuation was as much the norm in those days as consistency is in ours. Even the most fundamentalist scholar does not use, when quoting from an old text, the long *s*'s. Nor does he treat us to the eighteenth-century letter writing convention of anticipating on the bottom of one page the first word of the next. If sense is in any way affected by a modernization, that must of course be indicated.

turned impressively over a glowing sea of coals, giving off an aroma of roast meat delightful to a growing boy. There were speeches, and extended cheers for the projectors. We have sorely misread Jacob Dyckman's character if he did not, as his son watched, bask in the praise and glory, shout and shake hands. It was a never-to-be-forgotten moment — and it was to teach a bitter lesson.

Traffic rumbled over the Dyckman's Bridge while King's Bridge remained so empty that Philipse abandoned all effort to collect tolls. We may assume that the custom in Dyckman's tavern augmented. Yet all was not well in States's home. The citizenry had been glad to cheer and were delighted to make use of the free bridge, but the subscription to pay the costs was never completed.

After the bridge had been open a little more than a year, Jacob Dyckman, Palmer, and States's Uncle John informed the legislature that the outlay had been £830 and only £330 had been subscribed. They petitioned for permission to reimburse themselves with a lottery or by some other means. We can visualize the amusement elicited in the members of the ruling families at being asked to bail out peasants suffering the consequences of insubordination; the petition was denied. States's father sent in a personal plea, explaining that he was in desperate financial straits. No official hearts were warmed. If a child's mind was open to lessons in the imprudence of radical oppositions to established power, here was a good one. All the more, because another aspect of the situation cut deep into his own being. There was no more reason for the youth to call himself Staats. He anglicized his name to States. All hope of patronage from his rich namesake — and indeed, any of the patricians his father had cultivated — had been dispelled.

States was the fourth among ten brothers and sisters all of whom lived to maturity. In the anonymous middle of a large family, he established a passionately protective relationship with his sister Catalina, who was about thirteen years his junior. The family tavern was surrounded by a farm where the children labored. The shy, over-sensitive boy found the fields a refuge: although he was to make his stormy livelihood in cities, his perpetual dream was to save his money and settle down to quietude as a gentleman farmer. The most successful of his father's operations was the hereditary one of keeping an orchard. The Dyckman fruit trees became so famous that he shipped to the Crown's great Indian agent, Sir William Johnson, up the Mohawk River on the edge of the wilderness. When in deadly trouble, States was to find comfort in the purchase and nurture of delicate and fine fruit trees.

His father remained full of a vitality that must have humiliated a youth who was to grow up so obsessed with decorum. When States's oldest brother, Samson (Sampson), who kept a livery stable, was appointed a post rider, the father visualized himself also galloping glamorously through the countryside, a mailbag swung over his shoulder. Although almost fifty years old, he pulled political strings in an effort to get for himself an appointment like his son's. He did demonstrate acquaintance with leading men, but he could not persuade them.

States's father was always energetic and full of schemes. Yet the more schemes, the worse his finances. He drew so heavily on his own father that the old man considered he had anticipated his inheritance and left the family property to his younger brother, William, who eventually built the stone dwelling on 204th Street and Broadway which is now the Dyckman House Museum.

From the farmhouse and inn where States was growing older, furniture and decorations disappeared as they were to disappear, years later, from States's own home when he was driven to the edge of insanity by the necessity to sell off his assets publicly during the bitterest and unhappiest period of his life. Eventually, Jacob went completely under: he assigned all his property to his creditors. Trying to save the family dwelling, Samson took it over, but he could not keep it. He sold out when States was eighteen.

A year and a half later, on February 17, 1774, *Rivington's Gazette* announced, "Mr. Jacob Dyckman in returning home to Harlem from this city fell from his horse at the bottom of the hill below Mrs. McGown's and fractured his skull in such a manner that his life is despaired of."

An explanation of the sudden death of Jacob Dyckman was recorded by an antiquarian who heard it from Mrs. McGown's grandson, who in turn had been told it by his father:

Dyckman had stopped in at McGown's Tavern "as usual" for a drink, but the widow was in an angry mood. She upbraided him for having cheated her by selling her the property as unencumbered when actually there was a mortgage on it which she had been forced to pay. Dyckman tried to pass the matter off lightly, but Mrs. McGown would not be appeased. As he went out the door, she shouted after him, "The curse of the widow and orphans will follow you to your grave!" He mounted and was almost instantly pitched over the horse's head to his death.

There was no reason for the McGowns to suppress this tale, and there was never a story that was likely to move faster on the wings of gossip. What was the reaction of the twenty-year-old States concerning this addition to the far from triumphant saga of his father? He went through life conscious beyond excess of his public image among his neighbors, which typically he saw endangered.

CHAPTER TWO

༄

Arrest and Flight

STATES DYCKMAN was to harbor ambitions to be a writer. He built a handsome mansion, was proud of his "refined" taste, and during his lifetime collected two considerable libraries, the books sumptuously bound. Yet in his copious correspondence he never discussed esthetic or literary matters, and he showed himself ignorant of the "classical" knowledge in those days required of an educated man. The boy was undoubtedly — as was then the common practice for yeoman's sons — apprenticed at an early age. He must have been put with a merchant since he became expert at keeping and manipulating accounts.

His family was passionately wed to its own soil: even when uprooted by the Revolution, they moved the minimum distance moderate safety dictated. States shared the love for his corner of the earth — it always beckoned him — but he became an inveterate traveler. How he got to the far end of Hudson River navigation at Albany we do not know, but it is clear that he was well-established there when he first emerges into the records at the age of twenty-two.

According to long established political and social hierarchies, Dyckman could hardly have been in more important company than the men with whom, in June, 1776, he drank "damnation to the enemies of the King." Present were the Royal Mayor of Albany, Abraham Cuyler; Stephen de Lancey, member of the most powerful New York family that remained loyal to the Crown and himself the possessor of a constellation of Crown offices; Benjamin Hilton, Albany's conservative sage; and others of the same stripe. States's presence beside them on that evening must have been more than chance since, long after they had all been blasted from the foundations which seemed so solid, his drinking companions remained close to him.

The youth from a simple background downriver, who had been taught a bitter lesson concerning the punishment meted out to those who opposed the status quo, had successfully ingratiated himself in Albany with those currently powerful. They were men of breeding and property, who lived elegantly, and States, who had known squalor, loved gracious and expensive living.

At this early stage, it was by no means clear that his association with such established leaders could be really dangerous. The Rebels would surely be put down, and in any case, the Revolutionaries belonged mostly to the class from which Dyckman hoped that he could, more effectively than his father, extricate himself. He had thus chosen sides for reasons, not political or ideological but of personal association and social taste. Dyckman never expressed, in his writings during the Revolution, devotion to the Crown or the British Empire. He did not even denounce the Rebel cause to which, indeed, most of his family adhered. (At almost the exact moment that he was being arrested in Albany, his brother Samson was employed by the New York Committee of Safety to summon suspected Tories for investigation.)

Dyckman had a strong streak of loyalty, if not to the Crown, to his friends; and he could be stubborn. All that was necessary for him to regain his liberty after his arrest at the birthday party was to sign "The New Association," which meant pledging support to the Continental Congress, etcetera. He refused and was sent back to jail. Two days later, the Committee of Correspondence included him in a list of those who could "go at large" if they would permit themselves to be disarmed, sign the Association, and give security that they would not roam around but stay in Albany. States's drinking companion Cluett accepted. States did not.

Before the week was out, the judges at the Mayor's Court applied to have Dyckman released from jail to appear before them. States "refused to come." The judges made no move to force him.

It has become fashionable for historians of the Revolution to dwell with iconoclastic zeal on atrocities visited on Loyalists. Such atrocities undoubtedly existed, but the treatment of Dyckman and his associates reveals that the principal emotion of the patriot authorities in Albany was embarrassment. What could they do about friends — often relatives — who had suddenly been transformed into potentially dangerous enemies?

The Tory "jail" where Dyckman and the others were lodged was a group of rooms in one of Albany's most elegant buildings: the state house. The Committee voted permission for "women, children, and fathers" to visit prisoners. Severity was limited to instructing the jailers not to let more than two of the prisoners out of the rooms at the same time and then "only when occasion required." There was no interior plumbing.

Since a British attack on New York was imminent, the Committee now voted that States's friends, Cuyler, de Lancey, and Hilton, be exiled to Hartford, Connecticut, at a safe distance from the expected fighting. States may well have been originally included in the order, since on the day it was promulgated, June 18, he reached an accommodation with the Committee. He still refused to sign the Association, but he gave his parole "not to correspond with any person or persons in order to dissuade or influence him or them against the measures pursued." He also agreed not to bear arms or leave Albany without permission. He was released until evening to raise bail. That he had the bail on the following day further reveals that the twenty-two-year-old businessman was well established in Albany.

The aftermath of the King's birthday party separated Dyckman from his more important Loyalist friends. On his own, he
did not get into any recorded trouble with patriot committees.
For months no record included his name. He was, we know,
somewhere in patriot territory. Perhaps he was held by his
parole in Albany. However, the familiarity he exhibited, when
serving the British, with the small details of life in Westchester
County seems to indicate that he stayed inconspicuously with
members of his family there.

Wherever he found refuge, Dyckman was no more than a distant observer of the stirring events that were taking place. A few
days before the Continental Congress adopted the Declaration of
Independence, the British began sailing into New York Harbor.
When Dyckman received news that the Crown had sent a tremendous army protected by an invincible fleet, his Tory proclivities were surely pleased. But he could not realize that the size
and complication of what was, in fact, the largest expeditionary
force of the entire eighteenth century would open for him a career that continued for the rest of his life and would make him
two fortunes.

In August, the British captured the essential American fort on
Brooklyn Heights. In September, they crossed the East River to
land on Manhattan about halfway between the city and the village of Harlem. Washington's army was forced to flee to the
northern tip of the island. He fortified a high, extensive cliff
called Harlem Heights and kept troops encamped on the old
Dyckman property to protect his escape possibilities to the rest
of the continent: King's Bridge and the bridge that sometimes
bore the Dyckman name. However, in October, the British
made Washington's position untenable by sailing up Long Island
Sound and landing on the mainland above Manhattan. The
Americans evacuated all the island except for Fort Washington
on Harlem Heights. During November the fort fell, and Washington's army crossed the Hudson River in the hope that they

could block the roads through New Jersey to the patriot capital, Philadelphia. Following Washington, the British abandoned, for the rest of the war as it proved, any concerted effort to move their lines farther north in New York, overrunning the Dyckman family's new haven in Westchester.

Still in Rebel territory Dyckman had every reason to be pleased with his choice of sides and the progress of the war. As Washington was driven, like a hare helpless before powerful hounds, across New Jersey, the inhabitants of that state flocked to swear renewed allegiance to the Crown. Their actions seemed proof of what the Loyalists and the British government had all along contended: the Revolution was nothing more than a plot staged by a few incendiary terrorists: drive the terrorists away, and the people would eagerly return to their old government. It followed that the rebellion could be extinguished by expelling the agitators systematically, from one state after another, establishing in each area garrisons that would cooperate with His Majesty's loyal subjects in repelling any efforts of the troublemakers to return.

But in early winter, as Dyckman tried not to smile visibly at the glum faces around him, disturbing cheers sounded. Washington had crossed the Delaware and annihilated a Hessian post at Trenton. It seemed rational, when Dyckman was in secret conclave with other Tories, to laugh this off as a mere flea-bite, but then there came a deluge of bad news. Washington had gone on to pick off two British regiments at Princeton. The inhabitants of New Jersey were tearing up their certificates of allegiance and harassing the retreating redcoats. Most of New Jersey was recaptured by the enemy. It became manifest to Dyckman as to everyone that this was going to be a long war.

Early in January, 1777, Dyckman kept a rendezvous at the Hudson River village of Fishkill with the deposed mayor of Albany, Abraham Cuyler. After breaking his parole at Hartford,

Cuyler had been hiding out in Rebel territory. The two men decided to "escape" to the British encampment in New York. The distance was about fifty miles and, it being January, there was snow on the ground. Unless they were fortunate enough to go by boat, they traversed, surely on horseback, what was in effect a no-man's-land. The British had not considered it worthwhile to do more than mount an occasional foraging raid into Westchester, and the patriot authorities were unable to keep order. Who was a patriot and who a Tory was so confused that robber bands circulated, pretending to be one or the other, and falling on inhabitants almost at random. The appearance of strangers on the glimmering snowy roads inspired in the inhabitants not curiosity but terror: Dyckman and Cuyler heard bolts thrown, saw lights extinguished. If they themselves became conscious of the approach of other riders, who might be bandits or Rebel committeemen, they galloped into the woods.

At last, the two fleeing men were challenged by a sentry in reassuring British tones. There was undoubtedly a flurry about identification, but Cuyler was well-known. States was allowed to proceed south through the familiar roads of upper Manhattan. How interesting to see that McGown's Pass, where he had been born, now bristled with fortifications.

New York was an entirely different city from that which Dyckman had known as a boy and a young man. A considerable area was rubble, for there had been a great fire, and the ruins were made doubly sinister by the fact that they were inhabited. Many American refugees who had come to New York loyally and proudly to support their King, were living in utter poverty in roofless, burned-out rooms. Their daughters, who should have been spinning by snug fireplaces at home, were receiving one lobsterback every twenty minutes to earn some cash for food. All around him Dyckman saw twin phenomena with which he was utterly unfamiliar: extreme poverty and extreme luxury. How the youth, who was always to have a passionate eye for such things, stared at the fine carriages which moved down the streets behind four horses! How he admired the marvelous clothes of the women — often, as he was to learn, officers' mistresses — more elegant than anything he had ever imagined. Then his attention was drawn away by a woman in rags clawing in the gutter for a loaf of bread.

The city was under the military government of an army from overseas, and the overlords did not let themselves suffer from the acute shortage of food, firewood, housing. Band music sounded. Everywhere there were uniforms. The military Dyckman saw were thus described by the painter William Dunlap: "Here was . . . the flower and pick of the English army. Here was to be seen a party of the 42nd Highlanders in national costume, and there a regiment of Hessians, their dress and arms a perfect contrast with the first. The slaves of Anspach and Waldeck were there — the first somber as night, the second gaudy as noon. Here dashed a party of the 17th Dragoons, and there scampered a company of Jaegers. The trim, neat, and graceful English grenadier, the careless and half-savage highlander with his flowing robes and naked knees, the immovable stiff German could hardly be taken as part of the same army." But in their attitudes towards the refugees they were alike. If Dyckman, in his travel-soiled American clothes, met any soldier in the street, he had to step into the gutter lest he be pushed there.

Dyckman was terrified by the inhuman human machine to which he had with the highest hopes and a loyal heart fled. It took him some time to realize that he was no longer "one whom fortune had neglected."

CHAPTER THREE

❧

Hidden Fountains of Gold

THE secret to bearable life in the occupied city was to establish a link with the British power. Dyckman was hired at once by the Quartermaster Department: he may well have been surreptitiously recruited when still on the American side of the lines. His "local knowledge and connection," he was to explain, enabled him "to be of the utmost service."

The quartermaster's principal function was to provide inland transport for the supplies and all the complicated equipment of an up-to-date European military force. Dyckman's hiring coincided with a major crisis in the procurement of the necessary wagons and horses.

During 1775, the British regiments in Boston, having nothing to gain by advancing inland through fields automatically fortified with stone walls, found little need for the transport. In 1776, from the time a greatly augmented army had landed in New York Harbor through the Battle of Brooklyn Heights, the conquest of New York City and on through the Battle of White Plains to the capture of Fort Washington, the soldiers had operated near enough deep water to be easily supplied from naval provision ships. During the subsequent advance through New Jersey to the Delaware, Washington's army had been in such abject flight that the quartermaster officers had merely to ask the terrified inhabitants for horses and wagons in order to get

[25]

what they wanted at their own price. But Washington's victories at Trenton and Princeton and the subsequent British withdrawal from most of New Jersey had reversed the situation. Now, as the quartermasters complained, "every kind of inveteracy" was so raising its head that no dependence was to be placed on normal methods of procuring horses and wagons.

The British, who had till then been sure that most Americans were on their side, had not foreseen any such situation. Thus, they had not worried about exhausting the wagons and horses in the territory they held permanently: Staten Island, Manhattan, and part of Long Island. Wagons and horses would somehow have to be procured from territory controlled by the Rebels.

Mounting military raids did not suffice, since patriot informants moved more quickly than British regulars, and teams could vanish in a jiffy. The necessary would have to be bought secretly from farmers who were risking severe penalties, and then spirited away under the very noses of the Rebel committeemen. Everyone who played a role in this dangerous process could count on being well paid. The feebleness of government and resulting general confusion in Westchester County presented great possibilities to an agent who knew his way around. Dyckman was highly familiar with the region and the persons in it.

The quartermasters could hardly post notices at crossroads announcing that they would pay well for wagons. States's knowledge of who was a Loyalist and who was in serious financial difficulties was an extremely valuable asset as was his familiarity with back roads and inconspicuous beaches. A team seemingly rolling along on farm business or moving almost invisibly through a dark night could meet up with a platoon of British soldiers or a boat come ashore in any of the innumerable coves along the banks of Long Island Sound or Hudson River.

Whether or not Dyckman himself crossed the lines to knock on doors at midnight cannot be ascertained — the essence of covert activities is to keep no records — but it seems most improbable. Physical derring-do was not his forte and, now that he was known to be in the British employ, he would have had to wear a disguise. He undoubtedly laid plans in New York City that would be executed by agents he had recruited.

Dyckman's activities in suborning wagons and the large sums he earned thereby were to one side of his regular duties and his established salary. He was hired to be a clerk, an accountant. As an American used to provincial mores, he could only have been amazed at the financial practices of the quartermaster corps. (Even the sophisticated Franklin had been amazed by a similar discovery.) The quartermasters, like all the officials around them, received only token salaries. It was understood that the true reimbursement came from putting in their own pockets a considerable part of the monies they expended for the Crown. This was done from department to department by different means. The quartermasters had their own particularly lucrative expedient.

It had all begun in 1755, during the French and Indian War, when General Edward Braddock was sent from England with two regiments to march across the Alleghenies and drive the French from Fort Duquesne (now Pittsburgh). As he tried to organize the expedition on the brink of the wilderness, Braddock found that he could not procure the transport needed to carry the supplies and artillery of a sophisticated army over the mountains. Farmers were unwilling to let their wagons and horses out of sight, and they had no desire themselves to accompany the army into the Indian-infested wilderness. Teams that the British reached for disappeared from view.

Braddock ruled that it would be too expensive for the army to buy the necessary wagons, particularly as the campaign was scheduled to be short (although not as short as it actually proved). The matter was solved efficiently and surreptitiously. The quartermaster officials personally bought horses and wagons which they, in their public capacity, rented from themselves. This enabled the army to move to its disastrous rendezvous with the Indians.*

The precedent established by Braddock, that the quartermasters own the horses and wagons which they rented from themselves, had become for the British army in America established practice. However, no hint of this practice, which opened up to the quartermasters tremendous opportunities for profits, was allowed to appear in the official accounts which it was part of Dyckman's function to keep.

Twenty-two years had passed since Braddock had abandoned trying to hire individual carters with their teams, yet the continuance of such hiring was assumed. Although the "establishment" was now "permanent," wagons were paid for by the day, and, as far as the books revealed, the hire for each was paid in full individually to each driver. The vouchers on which the whole system rested consisted of names for the drivers, statements as to the size of the wagons, and attestations, presumably signed by each driver separately, that the hire had been paid. Many of the signatures were merely the marks of men incapable of writing their names. Since the quartermasters owned and would protect the property, the carters could be the simplest of people. They were often slaves rented out by their owners.

The fascinating aspect of this method was that, although it enabled the compilation of impressive lists, it presented to scrutiny an impenetrable surface. The putative drivers were such inconspicuous and therefore untraceable individuals that the addition of imaginary names to account for nonexistent wagons could

---

* Benjamin Franklin had helped out, raising wagons and horses in Pennsylvania. He was given some money by Braddock but spent more. When he tried to collect the difference from Braddock's successor, Lord Loudoun, His Lordship indicated his assumption that Franklin had already found ways for more than paying himself. "I assured him that was not my case, and that I had not pocketed a farthing; he appeared clearly not to believe me; and, indeed, I have since learned" — so Franklin continued in his autobiography — "that immense fortunes are often made in such employments."

never be detected. (It was later suspected that a whole wagon train which had regularly been paid for had never existed.) And, of course, the authentic drivers whose signatures attested to the whole hire actually received only a pittance. How much? There was no way of telling. And who got the rest? The books gave not the slightest indication of who the actual proprietors were.

At the beginning of each quarter, the British commander in chief authorized the expenditure for the next three months: the calculation was a simple one; the number of horses and wagons which would make up the train was determined and then multiplied by established rentals.

At the end of the quarter, an abstract of the official accounts was presented to the commander in chief. Swamped by innumerable duties, after a quick glance to determine that the figures jibed in the main, he approved, conscious that the accounts would eventually be scrutinized by auditors in London. If discrepancies were then found, the quartermasters, who had personally received the funds, would be held responsible.

There was, of course, another set of books. They went to the mercantile house of Winthrop and Kemble, where the funds received from the commander in chief were also deposited. Here a true balance between intake and outlay was made, and the spoils were divided, in pre-determined proportion, among the proprietors. Dyckman was not supposed to be privy to this process yet he had sharp eyes and perceptive ears. He could not know how much the quartermasters were making but he was to conclude, when his view became larger, that their profit was at least three quarters of what the Crown was paying for the entire transport of the army. Whatever sums may have sprayed out sideways to important officials who needed to be propitiated, the body of the earnings went to the few very top officials. Dyckman could deduce percentages from what he was himself paid for his extra-official activities in this particular. Between January, 1777, and June, 1779, he received as "gifts" from Quartermaster General Sir William Erskine, £105, and from two deputies, William Sherriff and Henry Bruen, £52.10. apiece.

Let us not think in modern terms by regarding the total, £210, as an insignificant amount of money. It would come today to over $20,000,* and it was in addition to his earnings (obviously large though unrecorded) from the smuggling of horses and wagons, and his official salary.

As the property of the patriot members of the Dyckman family bled away in the endless confusion of Westchester, the Loyalist's pocketbook bulged. His favorite little sister, Catalina, felt "confined" in a countryside that lacked a dancing school. States persuaded their mother to allow her to live in New York City in his care. He set the girl up in style with a nurse and showered her with praise so extreme that, as the young girl complained to him, it was such as "I did not expect nor yet desire from a brother."

But States was too high-spirited a bachelor to have even a beloved sister live with him. Pat Conroy, whom he had helped secure profitable British business on Long Island, allowed him to see a confidential letter received from a young lady under stress. "I know," he explained, "anything new will be welcome to you."

---

*Because of the differences in relative costs of specific articles — glass and salt, for instance, were once very expensive and are now dirt cheap — and in ways of life — States never needed a television set or a washing machine — economic historians are extremely hesitant to generalize concerning equivalent values of money at different dates. Furthermore, as this is being written, the value of the dollar is plummeting to we know not what eventual level. But if a book like this is to make any sense, some guiding indication must be attempted. Although the outcomes are sometimes incongruous, and costs in America were lower than in Britain, I have concluded that it would be reasonable enough to calculate that one eighteenth-century pound equaled a hundred contemporary dollars. I have reached this figure, so obviously in round numbers, not by comparing the costs of any specific articles or groups of articles, but determining the incomes of people living in equivalent manners.

Shortly before the Revolution, John Singleton Copley wrote from Boston to his fellow painter Benjamin West in London, "You are sensible that 300 guineas a year, which is my present income, is a pretty living in America." This statement is one of those that make the proportion of one hundred to one seem too conservative: an extremely successful portrait painter would not today call some $30,000 annually "a pretty living."

Conroy did not expect Dyckman to visit Long Island since he had no "Dulcinea" there.

States had found a Dulcinea in New York City. Early in 1779, Eleanor Brewer gave birth to a boy whom she called States Dyckman Brewer. In a will Dyckman drew up two years later, he referred to the child as his godson, but established the new States as one of his two immediate heirs, co-equal with his mother.

There can be no doubt that States was riding high. He had no reason to feel either guilty or uneasy concerning the practices he was engaged in. Did he not serve his rightful King and help impoverished Loyalists trapped in Rebel territory when he arranged for the smuggling out of their teams? And looking around him in New York City, he saw all British officialdom extracting, in one way or another, extensive personal profits from their "preferments." If the quartermasters had an expedient, peculiar but traditional, so did many another department.

Dyckman had a very soft heart when it came to the difficulties of his relations and friends, but nothing is easier than to get accustomed to poverty when it characterizes not individuals but a class. The poor Loyalists vanished from his vision. New York, being a military camp, was much more directed than a peacetime city to a single end, and Dyckman, although a civilian, had an insight into the very core of the machine, more so indeed than many of the bedizened generals. Whatever was planned involved wagons and horses, and whatever involved wagons and horses, he knew. He was extremely grateful to those who had on his arrival put him in this position and filled his pockets. He looked up to the quartermaster generals with a type of reverence unknown to democrats: he felt he was honoring himself by honoring them. And his superiors responded, finding him in his place and role as attractive as he was useful.

Physically, States Dyckman was a vertical man, tensed by taut nerves. His shoulders were very narrow. A long neck carried a long slender head up high. His hair, when not powdered, was dark, his eyebrows black arcs, his eyes turquoise, his nose long and shapely, his upper lip and chin long, his mouth tight. He was fastidious, elegantly dressed. Without any of the dry pomposity that often goes with ability to handle detail, he was reassuringly efficient. Tactful and courteous, he never gave any hint of a personal judgment on what he was asked to do. Happy with his duties and his rewards, he was humorous, able to relax into a warm but unobtrusive conviviality. In sum, he had the gift of being one of the most ingratiating of men. He was a pleasure to have around the office. As remained the case with Americans in British society down the years, his nationality permitted his superiors to indulge in an agreeable friendliness which would have been impossible with inferiors of their own nationality — that was as long as States did not presume. States did not presume.

Class distinction did not separate Dyckman too greatly from his original employer and immediate superior, Lieutenant Colonel William Sherriff. That Sherriff was one of the English officers who had served longest and most steadily in America did not testify to the influence of his family or to his own enterprise. He had been doing garrison duty in the colonies before the French and Indian War. Having taken an undistinguished part in that conflict, he stayed on while all his fellow soldiers of position and ambition returned to their native shores. In 1768, Sherriff became deputy quartermaster general. The profits to be earned from scattered garrisons in a distant land being too small to attract any Englishman of importance, no full quartermaster general was sent in over Sherriff's head. Things did heat up when the Revolution approached, but even after actual fighting had broken out in 1775, the British expected to extinguish the uprising with a few puffs of powder. Sherriff was not at once superseded. An indignant Tory tells us that, when the menace of Washington's cannon drove the British out of Boston, 150 hogsheads of rum were "part only of the plunder" which Sherriff loaded, to the exclusion of the legitimate possessions of the Tory refugees, on the boats that carried the British army to Halifax.

When the Crown, persuaded that strong military action was necessary, sent over its huge expeditionary force, the office of quartermaster general offered too many perquisites to be left to an obscure soldier like Sherriff. The commander in chief, Sir William Howe, steered the appointment to his friend, the cavalryman Sir William Erskine, who was considered by some the most effective of all the British combat commanders. Howe, of course, did not intend to divert so valuable a soldier from his military duties, but rather to reward them. Erskine, although he was to play the most determining role of any man in Dyckman's life, was not normally seen around the office.

The son and grandson of active combat officers, General Erskine had fought at the age of seventeen in the Battle of Fontenoy (1745). He was to remain in the army for fifty-three years, fighting through nineteen campaigns in America, Germany, and Flanders, to become a lieutenant general. He was in essence a cavalryman.

At first, Dyckman may well have had difficulty understanding what his superior said: in a service crowded with Scots, Sir William was conspicuous for the heaviness of his brogue. He was deeply rooted in the Scottish aristocracy and, when not on campaign, settled down devotedly in the Scottish countryside. Torrie, his ancestral mansion, was on the Firth of Forth, at the opposite end of the Bay of Culross from the castle of his cousin, the Earl of Culross. The family controlled that center of fishing and conveying goods across the Firth.

Now in his fifties, Sir William was muscular, tall, broad, and heavy. On a neck so short and thick that it seemed hardly to rise from his shoulders, he had a tremendous heart-shaped head: the broad, low dome expanding outward to very full fleshy cheeks which gave way to an inward curve that, after passing the broad mouth, narrowed to a long, almost pointed, chin. His eyes seemed tiny in comparison with his tremendous nose with its conspicuous nostrils. An ugly face, entirely suited, so it seemed at first glance, to a brute on horseback, such a condottiere as once ravaged the Italian countryside. Yet the little eyes were gentle. When not on martial duties, Sir William was bashful and unaggressive. In an army where almost every high officer was feuding with the others for power and perquisites, Erskine was universally popular. He developed an almost fatherly feeling for the up-tight, narrowly built clerk who carried his own nervousness and insecurity with his own type of gallantry.

A man of the sword, not of the countinghouse, more feudal in his approach than mercantile, Sir William was glad to take what perquisites came to him naturally, but it was not in his character to behave, as he visualized, meanly. Just as Dyckman was starting in the Department, Erskine recommended to Howe that private ownership of the army transport be abolished. The wagon train and the supply boats should be purchased "on government account."

The other quartermaster officials could not have been too pleased, although they would not have been expropriated. The government would have had to buy their teams, as the only ones available in adequate quantity. Having a virtual monopoly, mysterious proprietors could demand of themselves a high price. However, the issue did not arise. The commander in chief objected that purchasing "would lead to expenses which could never be ascertained." He was the more chary because a government-owned train which had been imported from England at vast expense — some £100,000 — had come to nothing: the horses had died or become sickly on the transatlantic voyage, and the wagons proved too heavy for American roads. Howe was unwilling to upset the existing system of rental, which functioned effectively and gave him a solid figure to budget.

Erskine did not argue. Not only was the existing system to his financial advantage, but allowing things to proceed as usual meant that he could, while in good conscience collecting the emoluments, leave the bother to his deputies. When later investigated in England, he contended that he could not be held responsible for what went on behind the scenes: "His duties in the field, where he was once for five months together, and the variety, multiplicity of his military business, and the many detachments he was sent out with, rendered it hardly possible for him to attend to the accounts, and to the manner of conducting the money transactions; and therefore he does not know much further than what appears on the face of the vouchers."

With the return of the clement weather in which European armies operated, General Howe tried to lure Washington down from heights near Morristown which the British considered too secure for attack but which commanded the road across New Jersey to Philadelphia. Since Washington would not oblige, an ocean voyage became necessary. Leaving behind an adequate garrison to protect his New York base — and the quartermaster offices with Dyckman in attendance — Howe embarked his army. They landed at the head of Chesapeake Bay, brushed Washington aside at the Battle of Brandywine, and took Philadelphia.

Word came back to New York that the British officers were having a wonderful time with the belles of America's largest and most sophisticated city, but the possession of the capital did not bestow the military advantages that would have been gleaned had America been as centrally and tightly organized as a European nation. Enemy activity flowed around the city, which became, in fact, a luxurious prison guarded by rebel guerrilla fighters. The enemy were operating so effectively that a major British force coming down from Canada under General Burgoyne was forced to surrender at Saratoga.

During the following winter, while the Rebels starved at Valley Forge, States lived high as an army employee in New York

City. However, the serenity of the Department was upset when orders came in replacing as commander in chief the easygoing Howe with his second in command, the neurotic and perpetually disgruntled Sir Henry Clinton.

Clinton summoned Erskine, and induced him to admit that he himself was one of the proprietors of the wagon train. The commander in chief then stated that "it sounded odd that the contract and the contract[or]s should be in the same hands."

Erskine put forward contentions that were down the decades to be rehearsed again and again in order to justify the quartermasters' doubling as proprietors: The practice had long been established in America, where the inhabitants were chronically unwilling to rent to the army their teams accompanied by their own services as drivers. Having a self-renewing succession of proprietors altogether in the British interest enabled an unfluctuating supply of wagons — no desertions after a defeat — and the maintenance of a uniform rental as established by the commander in chief not subject to profiteering when teams were hard to come by. Owning the wagon trains themselves, the quartermasters had both a double reason and double authority for making sure that the trains were efficiently maintained by able superintendents. Erskine induced Clinton to acknowledge what remained down the years the trump card of the quartermaster-proprietors: the train was consistently administered with "zeal, ability, and exertion."

Clinton had to agree that it would be foolhardy to change in the middle of a war an organization that was functioning effectively. Finally the commander in chief stated that, although he still thought the situation "odd," he should take no notice of it, but that Sir William Erskine "must at some future day be responsible."

This threat would be the springboard of Dyckman's career. But not immediately.

France had now entered the war against England. This expansion of hostilities forced the diversion of some of the British army in America to the protection of other British possessions in the hemisphere. Thus weakened, Clinton decided to abandon Philadelphia. In June, 1778, the occupying force marched for New York across New Jersey.

Tempted by the length of the British column — the wagon train by itself occupied twelve miles of road — the Americans attacked the British left flank at Monmouth. Had Washington succeeded in his objective of capturing the wagons, the proprietors would not have been desolated. They would have been reimbursed, at exalted valuations, for what was lost, and renewed the hire with replacements. However, the train galloped off during a British counterattack. The engagement eventuated in a pitched battle. Retrained during their winter at Valley Forge, the enemy amazed the British command by proving effective where they had formerly been at a great disadvantage: at hand-to-hand fighting. The British were forced to withdraw, leaving the Rebels in possession of the field of battle.

After most of the British army had safely reached their New York base, Clinton, his force weakened and the enemy more formidable, abandoned any effort to smash the Continental Army. Instead, he slammed shut the gates. Dyckman and the other inhabitants had no reason to fear that Washington, unassisted, would try to come in over the ramparts. But there was cause for anxiety when a French fleet, commanded by the Count d'Estaing, emerged from the ocean and anchored outside New York Harbor. Perhaps the warships, propelled by a strong tail wind, would come charging up the bay and sink the weaker British flotilla at its anchorage. Then French marines would land on the southern tip of the island while, to the north, Washington would come storming across the Harlem River onto the old Dyckman property and on into the city. But the French sailed off for

Rhode Island, and were soon driven entirely out of American waters by British naval reinforcements.

Militarily, the winter of 1778–1779 was quiet, yet Dyckman's tasks went on. The wagon train had, as the army grew in total smaller, been somewhat reduced, but there were still plenty of teams and horses to keep account of (and get paid for): enough to supply the needs and the staff and the artillery, and to carry at call twenty-one days' provisions for 10,000 men.

The exalted Sir William Erskine was becoming increasingly dissatisfied. According to the Hessian quartermaster general, Carl Leopold Bauermeister, Erskine finally listened to his friends who insisted that it was ridiculous for such a man as he to be involved in accounts that perpetually kept him late for supper. More probably, the lifelong warrior felt frustrated by the stalemate which continued to engulf the American war.

Erskine could not enjoy serving under Clinton, whom he disliked. And a proud man finds it irksome to operate in a manner which he had been warned might publicly be declared improper. The time was at hand when the authorities in London would audit his bills. Having given the business little attention, he would need help in organizing the accounts he would present to the authorities.

During the summer of 1779, Dyckman received the invitation that was to determine the rest of his career. He was to sail for England in the service and under the protection of Sir William Erskine.

CHAPTER FOUR

The Loyalist
Reaches London

DYCKMAN's sophisticated friend Benjamin Hilton feared that the American yeoman's son did not understand how great was his good fortune, or how to use it to advantage. "You are now, my dear friend . . . ," Hilton admonished, "going to mix with the great world, happily under the patronage of one who has it in his power to make your fortune. . . . I need not tell you to make the best use of your future time, and not only to command Sir William's friendship, but also to merit his love and esteem — the steps to effect this your own prudence will suggest to you. At all times to please and be contented, to study his foibles, etc., to flatter them may perhaps be no small ingredient to effect so desirable an end. That he may do by you in the same proportion, I wish."

Other indications hurried in. Stephen de Lancey, a scion of the patroons against whose insolent power States's father had helplessly beat his wings, begged the son for help. He sent States a list of what had been, before he had been unseated by the Rebels, his emolument in Albany as clerk of the Court of Common Pleas, clerk of the Mayor's Court, clerk of the Court of General Sessions, prosecutor on the part of the Crown, clerk of the County Records, and Surrogate: an annual total of £775. He wished a new commission that would recompense his losses. He would not himself have dared to make "so free as to have asked Sr Wm Arskin [*sic*] to befriend me in this." But the yeoman's son was now better placed. "Perhaps an opportunity may offer before you reach England to mention it to him."

Since the rulings on Erskine's accounts would determine whether all the quartermasters could keep their gains, it was agreed that Dyckman should still receive his official salary. But he would not need the money in London, where his patron would assume all his expenses. He asked a fellow clerk in the Department, Hugh Cairns, to receive the stipend and give Catalina so much spending money that she would be a very rich little girl. She was herself to control a dollar a day. The other half of States's salary was to defray her schooling expenses and pay some debts Dyckman would leave behind. His profits from a sloop he owned with Cairns (and rented to the Quartermaster Department) were to be saved, unless one of States's brothers came into the British zone, or Catalina asked for more money because of sickness or "any other cause." It is clear that States was so spoiling his little sister to keep her from joining their mother in Rebel-held territory, where he could not reach her when he returned or easily communicate with her in his absence.

As autumn approached, States sailed in a convoy which, although protected by warships presumed to be strong enough to defy Rebel privateers and French frigates, took the shortest possible ocean crossing: to Cork, in Ireland. The various vessels carried all the important British soldiers and officials who, in the fall of 1779, wanted well-protected passage for home before the gales of winter. As a member of Erskine's suite, States for the first time took part in grand entertainments of the wellborn and mighty. By nature shy, he was glad to stand in a corner as an observer, and he had no reason to feel that he was being awkward or conspicuous in that role. The role was suitable to a man in his station. Although he had the right of entry he was not supposed to presume by mingling with his betters.

On his arrival in August, Dyckman was the happy recipient of generosity. Erskine gave him ten guineas for new clothes and twelve more so that he could live extravagantly at an inn. Sir William intended to travel directly to London through Scotland, but States wanted to go off by himself. He wished to see Wales; Erskine compliantly agreed to pay his expenses, and Dyckman, a quick learner when it came to money, realized he was not expected to stint himself. He revealed a courtier's ability to accept munificent generosity munificently. Much of the way through Wales he traveled like a "milord" in a hired coach behind four horses to be greeted with obsequious bows at taverns a hundred times grander than those his father had been unable to keep afloat.

The only explanation we possess for States's private detour is contained in a letter to a Welsh lady in New York: Mrs. Williams. Her entrusting him with a message to her brother had inspired him with "the anxious desire . . . to see your native country."

Dyckman hoped to record in literary form his impressions of the Old World. He thanked a friend for his offer to preserve "my letters to allow me to re-peruse them at our meeting. At present, they are only to be considered as notes on which I mean to enlarge at my leisure. The method you recommend to me of making immediate memorandums I find very useful — for though the memory may be infinite and capable of containing the ideas caused by all our senses and imagination, yet I find if I trust too much to mind it resembles a lumber room where everything is thrown in promiscuously and where no particular thing can be found at the moment it is wanted."

States kept a copy of his letter to Mrs. Williams concerning Wales: "The grand ideas that delightful country raised in my mind can never be defaced. Nature seems here to have lavished all her magnificence as well as sweets — such a contrast I never expect to see again as that of the rugged mountains of Pennine and the enchanting valley of the Clue [Clwyd] — and what can exceed the beauties of the banks of the Dee! In fact, I am so much enamored of this earthly paradise that nothing but the connections I have in America could induce me to leave it."

As Dyckman neared London, he was excited by the prospect of finding awaiting him a letter from his young sister, Caty. None! Weeks passed and he became increasingly upset. Finally, he composed an appeal with such care that there are among his papers two preliminary drafts.

Sometimes, so he wrote his little sister, he imagined her "as perfectly satisfied and contented in your situation," but despite his "natural propensity to hope for the best," he was overcome with fears which "deprive me of my peace of mind." He was afraid that she had moved away from the British-held city where he had left her.

She should not conclude from "the style of letters" he had often written her that he was "discontented and gloomy. . . . I am as happy as it is possible for me to be at so great a distance from the source I draw all my happiness flows: to see you every day — to enjoy those pleasing walks when to promote each other's felicity was our mutual want, to watch and protect your youth and innocence from insult and danger, to anticipate your wants constituted my sole happiness when I was with you. There, recollect! You will forgive — can you blame me? — if my letters are sometimes too shaded with melancholy."

Here, both drafts break off to announce that he has at last heard from her and that she was still in New York. "Oh, my dear sister, how happy you have made me!

"So you think it not so pleasant . . . as when I was there? The trees do not offer so agreeable a shade, nor the bank of the river so pleasant a walk. You become leaner because you did not (bring) take with you one of my letters to feed upon. Tell me, was this meant to increase my love for you? If it were your *wish*, you have mistaken the means. . . . The tender manner in which you regret my absence" could not make him happy when her health was adversely affected. "You feed on my letters — they remind you of my being so great a distance from you . . . and that causes you to grow lean."

States jotted in one of his drafts a succession of incoherent phrases: "intense passion of my soul of my Soul Lord — just after our melancholy separation they can — communicate — there — said I dear to your soul and you cherish — I dear to your soul and you cherish them there — caress an . . ."

Despite the excision of these extreme expressions, his communications troubled as much as they fascinated Catalina. States was soon to hear that she had indeed moved to Rebel territory where she was indeed locked away from him.

Dyckman soon found London lodgings so satisfactory that he was to stay for years. His landlady was a Mrs. Tait. She seems to have been a widow who, after the death of her husband, took in, as lodgers, single genteel gentlemen. "The good Mrs. Tait," as she was often referred to by States's friends, made for the sensitive stranger a home. After States had recovered from a frightening illness, it was assumed that Mrs. Tait must be "out of her senses with joy." Dyckman was to pay for redecorating some of her rooms (perhaps those he himself occupied) and to make her a present of elegant china. Invitations often provided that he could bring Mrs. Tait along. Whether she was ever more than a substitute mother to him the copious references to her in the Dyckman Papers (which never reveal her first name) never make clear.

Mrs. Tait's connections formed the basis for Dyckman's easy association with native Englishmen. They were respectable members of the middle class; far lower in the social scale than Dyckman's patrons. Mrs. Tait's nephew, John W. Wintle, Jr., who became States's most intimate English friend, was a not-too-successful wine merchant in the provincial city of Newnham.

Dyckman was by nature flirtatious and, when occasion warranted, considerably more. In the manner of an eighteenth-century gentleman, he destroyed his amorous correspondence — with one exception. This exception was not an outburst of passion that would in rereading bolster up States's male ego. It tickled his funny bone. Penned charmingly in the coyest of female hands, devoid of punctuation, it mixed archness with spiteful jealousy and assigned a most equivocal role to the lady's husband:

Dr. Dykey

You have embarrassed me greatly by the very elegant present you was so obliging to bring me and Mr. H. still more so by repeatingly saying he would mention it to you which I still find he had not can you therefore forgive me begging now as a *particular favor* that you will suffer me to return it (having one entirely similar) it would be absurd to let anything so pretty remain useless and you must amongst your extensive acquaintance have many that may be fortunately like me in your esteem to one of them let me beg you to present it by this means you will have an opportunity of pleasing two — taking for granted that you will comply with my request I shall send it to your address and remain with the same regard and thanks
Dr Sir
Your sincere hubl servt
Anne Harris
Chelsea May 31

Girls must be found where they grow, but for male companionship States, like his fellow Loyalists in London, felt closest to other Americans. Untouched by the new continental point of view that was emerging among the embattled Rebels, the expatriots from each colony tended to huddle together. Dyckman frequented the New York Coffee House, where there were copies of the Tory newspapers published in the British-held city. Some of Mrs. Tait's rooms were often occupied by Loyalists States had known in Albany.

Dyckman's relationship with highborn Britons who were his patrons and employers exemplified customs almost unknown in his native America. When at home he had associated with members of the patroon class, the company had been, if only for the time being, all good fellows together. But aristocratic manners stemmed from the centuries when the residences of the great, built for defense, were so small and so thickly populated that the ramparts could all be manned at a sudden alarm. Where everyone was perpetually jostled in the narrow spaces with everyone else, an aristocrat did not notice the existence of inferiors except in direct relationship to their functions. Great ladies would take baths in the presence of footmen who were considered, in connection with highborn women, sexless.

In Dyckman's eighteenth century, a wide variety of ranks still ate at the master's table, but this physical propinquity did not breach the barriers of class. Although Sir William came to sign himself on letters to his young protégé "affectionately," Dyckman had to be careful. He was sometimes, in the great man's absence, entrusted with keeping track of the servants. They treated him with great deference, but their genuflections, however pleasing, had to be taken in the context of the total social situation.

After States had been in England about a year, he was encouraged by alcohol to assert his American-bred equality. "Ever anxious to oblige me," Erskine had insisted that States attend the races at Leith. Having been informed that only during the final days would "much company be present, which was all I wanted to see," Dyckman waited till then to make his appearance.

The horses ran along the seashore at low tide, the track being the half-mile of sand that was smoothed twice a day by the rising and receding of the waters. From booths erected on scaffolds, the entire tract could be surveyed. These booths were rented by groups of gentlemen who subscribed to have liquors and cold meats, along with waiters, sent from one of the hotels. Each subscriber was supposed to bring a guest, either a friend or an attractive stranger met beside the track. Traveling as usual alone, Dyckman presented a letter of introduction and was received. His hosts were not too obviously above the dapper stranger in rank. Everyone had a congenial time, and States was complimented and exhilarated by the attention of his new companions.

The exhilaration remained when, dining at one of the inns, he found himself surrounded "with dukes, earls, marquises, and lords." Going on to the theatre, he forgot, "my head being as light as a Frenchman's heels," what he had learned in England about social rank. "As I had assurance enough at that time to think myself qualified for any company, I tipped the doorkeeper and desired to be shown to the best seat, and was accordingly placed in the same row with Lord Haddington and Lord Ellebank. The latter I soon found a very conversable companion. He with great good nature pointed out all the ladies of birth and beauty to me; and finding me as little attentive to the play as himself, drew me into an argument on politick — the subject, the *Common Man*. In the midst of our conversation, the Duchess of Hamilton came in the same box, attended by seven ladies. We made room for Her Grace, and she happened to seat herself very nigh me on one side and my friend on the other. To my surprise, he resumed the conversation again. We were then joined by Lord Haddington, and talked so loud that the Duchess and her train, instead of attending to the action, were listening to us, probably because we could be heard most distinct."

Dyckman, who had "by this time pretty well recovered my reason," was overcome with embarrassment at being thus forced on the attention of so great a lady. It was "much to my satisfaction," when his interlocutor, Lord Ellebank, wandered away.

Dyckman, who had come to "see" rather than associate with the aristocrats, now sat happily silent, observing "the fair part of the audience particularly." Whether these fine ladies "received additional charm from the warmth of my imagination at that time I know not, but there was a natural glow on each cheek which no art could ever equal, and their fine, speaking eyes obliged my heart to confess them superior to all I had ever seen."

In stating his address, Dyckman sometimes wrote under 14 George Street, the direction "York Buildings," which was accurate, but at other times he substituted "Adelphi." York Buildings was a disparate group of houses, two to three stories high, some dating from the late seventeenth century. Nearby stood a veritable antiquity: the Watergate on the bank of the Thames which had been built in 1626 as the grand entrance to what was then a great ducal estate. This Jacobean structure, with its heavy masonry and ponderous decorative designs, fascinated antiquaries. But Dyckman was not one of those Americans who try to compensate for the newness of their native environments with a passion for antiquities. He yearned for what was most sophisticated of the up-to-date, and he had only to walk a few hundred steps from Mrs. Tait's door to enter the most ambitious and most celebrated eighteenth-century effort to create an elegant, unified urban environment: the Adelphi. Here the brothers Adam had exemplified their new, light and free, eclectic classical style in harmonious rows of buildings that lined both sides of the streets in horizontals varied but not shattered by decorative details.

The Loyalist far from his homeland, supported well by aspects of British society that were in many ways the most different from the American and against which his compatriots were actively rebelling, spent much of his time as a lonely stroller observing the men and particularly the women who made the society around him sparkle. Like a watcher of birds, he sought out places where they were likely to be seen. What better spot than the Adelphi's Royal Terrace! The settlement did not, it is true, attract aristocrats, who had their own great houses and were, like every established class, inherently scornful and resentful of innovation. The Adelphi attracted persons of advanced tastes and also those human sharks who swim through the teeming waters of the esthetically new. David Garrick died there at about the moment when Dyckman arrived: Boswell and Dr. Johnson enjoyed strolls on what Johnson eulogized as a peaceful backwater close to "the full tide of human existence at Charing Cross." The Royal Society of Arts occupied its mansion-headquarters (which still stands). There was another building, equally grand, whose entrance was decorated with discarded crutches. This was the Temple of Health operated by the celebrated quack James Graham. Whether or not States penetrated into the famous Apollo Room, the profusely decorated heart of the temple, he surely could not afford the Celestial Bed that rented at a hundred pounds a night and, through electricity, was guaranteed to have a most gratifying effect on the potency of the male. Inside, or as she passed along the street, States, with his proclivities, could hardly have failed to stare at the young girl — she was about fifteen — who played in the Temple the part of Goddess of Health. Did he prefer, to the charms of the aristocratic ladies that so bemused him, the glow of this daughter of the people who was to become one of the celebrated beauties in English history? She became Lady Hamilton and in the full light of public romance, mistress to Admiral Lord Nelson. Her innumerable portraits still enchant the male eye.

As he admired the true aristocrats, Dyckman could congratulate himself on his own role in nourishing all this glamour, grace, and glitter. Such extensive private emolument for public duties as he defended was basic to British aristocratic life.

The stability of titles and estates would break into bits were it not for entail, or, indeed, if the elder son who received all was obliged to dissipate the inheritance by supporting his younger brothers or his cousins in cadet branches. However, the broad gamut of aristocrats had to uphold their station by living expensively. They were forbidden to shatter class lines by joining the commonly born in trade. Therefore, sources of income had to be made available exclusively to the upper class. Gentlemen accepted appointments in the Church of England — ecclesiastical posts became frankly referred to as "livings" — or could serve the government more directly in civil office, or command in the army or navy. To attach adequate high salaries to these occupations would smack of commercialism and might agitate the taxpaying lower classes. In any case, a gentleman did not wish to receive money as if he were a tradesman,* or have anyone else tell him how much his services were worth.

According to Professor J. H. Plumb, Master of Christ College, Cambridge, "It was patronage that cemented the political system, held it together, and made it an almost impregnable citadel, impervious to defeat, indifferent to social change." Granting patronage, he pointed out, was more "than private charity." It was "power, and power is what men in politics are after."

Dyckman had intended — at least so he told his family and sometimes himself believed — to return to New York after a brief stay in London. A year had passed when he wrote that "maternal affection and brotherly love . . . though powerful at any other time," had now with him "no weight at all." He had held within himself "a court of inquiry on my return to New York in which *advantage* only was considered." True, if he returned he might be of service to his brothers "should any misfor-

---

*To pay fees to quasi-gentlemen, like doctors and solicitors, a special, less demeaning, financial designation was established, a guinea, worth one shilling more than a pound. But even guineas could not be handed directly to the recipient: they were laid down where he could with his own hands pick them up.

tunes happen to them or their families occasioned by the British troops." He might be able to persuade Catalina to return to her school in the city. Being present with the Quartermaster Department, he "might pick up some crumbs which fall from my Royal Master's table." But on the other hand, if the war were soon settled, he might be able in London "personally to solicit through my friend" a place in the renewed government of America. His income in New York, two shillings and sixpence a day, was mounting up in his absence. He dreaded a winter passage across the ocean. More important, "by staying till next year, I comply with the request of my patron and hope our friendship will take deeper root every day. Should Lord Cathcart or Captain Savage come over and bring their accounts with them, it would be to my interest as well as theirs for me to be here." Lord Cathcart had succeeded Sir William as head of the quartermaster general's office and Captain Savage was in trouble concerning the vast cost charged for a ship, the *Alarm Galley*, which, under the aegis of the Quartermaster Department, had been built in Newport Harbor.

On October 4, 1780, States wrote his mother. He began his letter with a plea to Rebel privateers: "Whos'ever's hands this may fall in, I hope will kindly permit it to pass, as it can injure no individual or community, but may be of the greatest consequence to an affectionate parent, my dear mother." Then he continued: "Since I saw you last, heaven, as if in compassion for what I feel in my mind from being separated from you and my dear brothers and sister, has indulged me with more than common health of the body. I have been detained longer in England than I expected, but I should certainly have returned last summer had my sister remained where I left her. I have now every hope that I shall be in New York next June, when, if I am still denied the pleasure of seeing you, I may have the satisfaction of frequently hearing from you — and if I am so happy on my return to hear you are still in health, it will be the greatest blessing heaven can bestow on your affectionate son."

He added a postscript: "Be under no anxiety for me. I have friends who have it equally in their power and inclination to serve me."

CHAPTER FIVE

♒

The Auditors of Imprest

Imprest was the term for monies advanced to soldiers, sailors, or public officials by the Crown. The Auditors of Imprest were assigned to determine whether such monies had been legitimately received, spent, accounted for. Sums which were disallowed would have to be returned, although without interest, by the recipients. Dyckman's task was to get the accounts of Erskine and Sherriff, the two quartermasters so far in London, approved by the Auditors of Imprest.

Although the investigation potentially threatened the fortunes acquired by the quartermasters, which they were already lavishly spending, the danger seemed slight. Dyckman had to handle what was only a routine audit, and such audits were not set up to embarrass high officials whose use of the perquisites of office contributed to the solidity of the British ruling class.

In their testimony to subsequent, more rigorous investigations, the auditors outlined their procedures. Despite the huge sums involved, justification was sought only in minuscule. Each wagon and team of horses continued to be viewed as independent from all the others and every day was considered separately. Assistant quartermasters out in the field had theoretically made interminable lists of the objects rented for the army at so much per diem, and, in each individual case, for so many days. The signature or mark of someone specified as the owner had attested for each payment. These lists had been presented in summary to secure the approval of the commander in chief. But now they were to be submitted in elaborate detail.

Later, when describing his services to Sir William's heir, Dyckman recalled that there had been "glaring errors and improper charges" under "contingencies" to the amount of £3,670.1.3. These he "rectified and saved." One example: he found "a private receipt" for a gift of 200 guineas to Andrew Dumford, an aide-de-camp. "It was altered and a grave error concealed. . . . There were receipts omitted to be signed and blank — till the account was put into my hands in London — to the amount of £2,000." The carelessness was not only in the small. "The receipts for the whole wagon line" were signed with the name Robert McGreggor, sometimes "in very good writing, the next quarter he writes hardly legibly, and the third quarter he forgets to write at all and makes his mark!"

Erskine had carried with him to America £20,000 sterling "under the idea that a *large* balance in his hands" would speed things up. To justify most of this sum, Dyckman was given only a "loose" pile of inadequate receipts, but a convincing accounting was necessary.

Finding almost as many errors as there were expenditures, Dyckman sent out letters asking for explanations, but the mails were slow and the results unsatisfactory. Thus George Stewart, who had been in charge at States's early stamping ground, Kingsbridge, wrote that he had already sent all the information he had and had subsequently "lost or mislaid the memorandums for which I selected such information." As far as he could remember, he had been responsible for six brigades of double wagons for foraging beyond the lines, five blacksmiths, three carriers, etc., etc., but he was not sure exactly what they had been paid. Another correspondent, who thanked Dyckman for his "condescension" in consulting him again, wrote that, as his answer to States's original request had been lost in the mails, he could cast no light.

The overall carelessness in justifying expenditures implies that Dyckman, the ever meticulous, had given in New York increasingly little attention to keeping accounts. The office had been small and the four clerks had clearly found more interesting and rewarding duties. But now a smooth surface had to be presented to the inquiring eye. Everything had to seem to make sense. Owners' names could not fly around like bits of paper in a whirlwind, nor could a small (two-horse) wagon expand to a big one (four-horse) and then shrink to its original size. Wagons might not appear and disappear like rabbits popping in and out of a burrow. Not only glaring errors but too general a confusion would, so Dyckman wrote when he was facing a more rigorous investigation, "have vitiated the whole accounts" even in "the old Auditor's Office where the examinations extended little further than comparing the receipts with the abstracts and counting the amount."

To an invitation to the country, States replied, "My situation is such that I must confine myself very closely to business for some time or perhaps displease a certain person who has it in his power to oblige me very especially, and, though prudence is but a secondary virtue, we must sacrifice pleasure to it or want in justice to ourselves. . . . But how shall I avert the vengeance of your sisters you threaten me with?" He requests his correspondent to "convince them that vengeance belongs only to the Gods — and the Goddesses spurned that power. Forgiveness becomes the softness of the sex much better. . . . Assure them that should I meet them with displeasure on their countenance, I should certainly not know them, as I have never seen them in that dress."

States would have been even more harried had the Auditors of Imprest bothered about which costs could legitimately be charged to the Crown and which were the responsibility of the wagons' owners. Although General Clinton had warned Erskine that he would have to justify the duality to the auditors, the accountants did not recognize — probably had not been informed — that the quartermasters and the proprietors were the same. They did not see that the officials had a personal interest in making the government pay for as much as possible. The auditors considered the acceptance of dubious bills no more than questionable judgment, and they could be counted on to respect the judgment of gentlemen in office — unless pulled up by too flagrant an example. Dyckman saw to it that no such example appeared.

While Erskine's and Sherriff's accounts were going routinely through the mill, Dyckman's clients were added to by the most powerful and the most toplofty of all: Lord Cathcart.

Sir Henry Clinton, while thinking it "odd" that the quartermasters should be the proprietors of the wagon train, had recognized a fruitful source of wealth. When Erskine resigned, he saw to it that the pot of gold would eventually devolve on "my most confidential friend," John Dalrymple. Although raised by Clinton from lieutenant colonel to the local rank (effective only in America) of major general, the appointee was a man of the conference table not the battlefield: he was being useful in England as Clinton's contact with Lord George Germain, the secretary of state for the American Colonies. Not wishing to break into the negotiations by summoning his emissary back to America, Clinton arranged that, until Dalrymple could take over, the twenty-four-year-old William Schaw, tenth Baron Cathcart, should be acting quartermaster general.

The Loyalist William Smith who, although the British chief justice in New York, was perpetually horrified by the goings on around him, wrote of Cathcart's appointment, "It does not please. He is so young, and so short-sighted as not to distinguish a man." But Cathcart was extremely handsome and very intelligent. He had entered the army two years before, and was now a major in the Light Dragoons. He was to rise in the peerage to become first Viscount and first Earl. In 1807, he served as commander in chief of the army in Denmark, capturing Copenhagen. By then he had been ambassador to Russia, a post his father had held before him. He is given considerable credit for engineering the cooperation between England, Russia, Austria and Prussia that humbled Napoleon. After Napoleon's defeat, he played a major role in the reorganization of Europe.

During his service in America, Cathcart was a leader among the highborn bucks in the British army. Having got a too influential Loyalist girl in trouble, he was (so gossip stated) forced to marry her. Her father, Andrew Elliot, was lieutenant governor. According to Smith, Elliot's appointment had been "the most unpopular, the most obnoxious, and the most disgusting of any one perhaps ever made in the Colony of New York." Smith considered Elliot the very prince of all the grafters and attributed to his influence Cathcart's appointment as acting quartermaster. The appointment also pleased in England.

After Dalrymple had taken over in New York during 1780, Cathcart appeared in London. But he did not, like States's previous clients, show any cordiality. He regarded the American as just another clerk doing what he was hired to do. States's patron, Erskine, considered himself much outranked by the nearsighted young man who moved in the most exalted social circles.

The nobleman's sister, Mary Cathcart Graham, was a great beauty (immortalized by Gainsborough) who presided over a select salon. His Loyalist wife achieved a close friendship with the Queen. At George III's court, Lord Cathcart made the effort that gave him a role in the history of American painting. The circle of influential Loyalists in London were outraged that the King's favorite painter and intimate companion was Pennsylvania-born Benjamin West, who frankly admitted his sympathy with the Rebels. In the presence of the King, Cathcart commented loudly to West that the British victory at Camden would not give the painter as much pleasure as it did His Majesty's *loyal* subjects. When West replied equally loudly that the calamities of his country never gave him pleasure, the company waited jubilantly for the King to expel him from court. But George III put his hand on West's shoulder: "Right, right, West. I honor you for it." Then he told Cathcart to remember that a man who did not preserve a love for his native land could not be a faithful subject to another.

The Auditors of Imprest remained compliant. The top official, Lord Mountstuart, was too highborn to do more than collect the emoluments of office. When the staff of his deputy, Charles Harris, found a flaw or inconsistency, Dyckman was queried specifically about that item. If he could not justify it, nothing more was done than refuse to allow that specific charge (no tide of suspicious misstatements having emerged). For the general probity of the accounts, so Harris was to explain, "reliance was on the oath originally administered to each accountant." They had all sworn, on first taking office, that they would religiously support the interests of the Crown.

Erskine was to testify that of the £600,698 presented on his personal account, only £801 was disallowed. Sherriff and Cathcart added that their accounts had met with "very few objections, mostly to small errors in calculation." In Sherriff's case, it had been necessary to substitute a new voucher for a defective one.

Normal procedure now required that each account, as passed by the auditors, "be engrossed upon parchment and upon paper," both copies going to the Chancellor of the Exchequer for a "declaration," to be signed by him and afterward by two Lords of the Treasury. Then the copy on paper was to be kept in the office of the auditor; that on parchment would go through the offices of the King's Remembrancer and the Treasurer's Remembrancer to the Pipe Office (from whence the quietus was to be issued) and where the parchment would remain.

[57]

Erskine, Sherriff, and Cathcart waited eagerly for the "quietus" which would signify that their profits were forever their own. But —

But the copies of the audits, those grandly on parchment or less grandly on paper, failed to get past the Chancellor of the Exchequer — or was it the Lords of the Treasury? Official ears did not have to be very sharp to hear an ominous rumbling in the clubs where national leaders met, and in the publications that brought the people at large to some extent into the political process.

The war was going badly. Now that France and Spain had become belligerents, now that the conflict had to be fought globally, England's resources were being severely tried. Taxes were rising. And in the ungrateful American colonies, those instigators of the whole trouble, there were no signs that the pestiferous Rebels, seemingly so insignificant a foe, were being successfully subdued. True, there had been since Burgoyne's surrender no major British defeats, and there had been some victories — Charleston, South Carolina, had been captured during May, 1780 — yet the rebellion went on as inveterate as ever.

An unsuccessful war is scanned more critically than a triumphant one. Public outrage at the money that was flowing away in America had fastened on the "extraordinary services": those departments where expenditures were not determined by budget but by the commander in chief, since costs presumably depended on the incidents of each campaign. Although these services included the barrack master, the engineer, and the commissary of stores and provisions, the expenditures of the quartermaster had most caught the public eye.

Rumors circulated in knowing circles "of imposition and of much wealth acquired during short service upon slender appointments." Dyckman's clients had not been hesitant or secretive in spending the wealth that had poured in upon them. Although a bachelor in lodgings, Dyckman was receiving from Erskine some sixty pounds a month for expenses (perhaps $6,000 in modern currency). His was not a saving disposition, and he had an ostentatious love for fine clothes and impressive equipage. That the American immigrant from the bumptious revolting colonies presumed to live so far above his rank as a clerk may well have added to the general disapproval. When aristocracy had been in its fullest flower, States would have been thrown in jail for being accoutered in a manner unsuited to his station.

Responsive to the "voice of the nation," Parliament passed an act empowering the nation's most puissant watchdogs, "The Commissioners Appointed to Examine the Public Accounts of the Kingdom," to investigate the extraordinary services. The Lords of the Treasury were not amused at Parliament's interference. They ordered their Commissioner of Accounts in New York, Major Duncan Drummond, to mount an investigation there. Surrounded in the British base with higher officers who might be implicated, Drummond dragged his feet. And Parliament's watchdogs at the moment were following another scent.

While the two investigations hung fire, what was in the long run to become the most serious menace to the quartermasters was raising its head in America. Getting nowhere in the North, where his force was countered by Washington's Continental Army, Clinton had decided to use captured Charleston as the base for a campaign against the more vulnerable South. This required dividing the British force. Himself sailing back to New York, Clinton had to entrust the southern army to his second in command, Lord Cornwallis. As Clinton had intrigued to replace his superior, Howe, Cornwallis was intriguing against Clinton. The two top officers hated each other.

Conscious that the expenses Clinton was countenancing were under criticism in London, having now the powers of an independent commander, Cornwallis established a money-saving method to secure supplies for the troops which Clinton was angrily to claim had been his own idea. And on December 30, 1780, Cornwallis announced with an obvious insinuation against Clinton, that "since I consider myself a steward of the public money . . . bound by the duty I owe my country to regulate the charges," his quartermaster was no longer to incur extravagant and unnecessary expenses by hiring the wagon train. He was to purchase it for the government, with the quartermaster charging no more than he actually paid out.

This was not in itself a serious financial blow for the quarter-master-proprietors. Advancing aggressively, Cornwallis could not collect a wagon train from individual inhabitants. He had to buy the existing train at a price the owners would accept. Fortunately, he had not raised the question of who were, in fact, those owners. Yet the practice of hiring that had been and remained essential to continuing profits was now being publicly challenged. Worse than that: the quartermaster's expenditures, so far an issue of only minor importance, were becoming involved in the feud between the two highest military officers in America, each with extremely important political connections.

As 1780 gave way to 1781, Cornwallis was still rampaging around the South, marching pretty well where he pleased but leaving behind no permanent effects: it was as if he were walking through water. He did rout General Horatio Gates at Camden, but new, more effective resistance was being organized by General Nathanael Greene. Clinton, still immured in his New York base, had placed his hopes on suborning treason: Benedict Arnold would hand over West Point, enabling the British to cut the rebellion in half through their control of the Hudson. But the plot was discovered;* still no real progress, while gold still flowed in a thick stream from His Majesty's Treasury!

---

*The involvement of Dyckman's brother in the crisis detonated by the discovery of Arnold's treason and the traitor's escape to the British, was thus described by Governor George Clinton of New York State in a letter to Washington written early on the following morning: "Samson Dyckman, on Arnold's application, recommended to him some

The parliamentary watchdogs ominously lifted their heads in the direction of the Quartermasters' Department, even taking some preliminary testimony. Obviously, Dyckman and his clients should get the other investigation, that ordered by the Treasury in New York, completed first. A favorable report could be foreseen: Major Duncan Drummond, who would conduct the investigation, had been Clinton's aide-de-camp; the board of officers before whom the matter would be tried would be appointed by Clinton; and Clinton's interest had become firmly attached to the quartermasters'. Not only was the incumbent, General Dalrymple, Clinton's personal appointment and intimate friend, but Cornwallis's public criticism had put Clinton publicly on the defensive.

Drummond, although he still felt he was being pushed into an impossible position, was persuaded to go ahead. It was hoped that his findings, given weight by a ruling of an army board, could be used to blunt attacks in London. As Drummond was to put it, "When I reflect that the Commissioners of Public Accounts are on the point of examining into the extraordinaries of the American War, and the probability there is of their calling upon the Lords Commissioners of his Majesty's Treasury for information on so intricate a subject, I own it stimulates my endeavors to give them all the light and explanation I am able to offer."

That the cards were to a considerable extent stacked did not

---

well affected persons in Westchester County from whom he might be most likely to obtain intelligence of the movement of the enemy. On hearing of Arnold's treachery, he determined to go down to the Highlands and obtain assistance to bring off the persons he recommended lest Arnold should report their names and have them taken off by the enemy. As I thought it wrong that any person employed by Arnold should be seen in that quarter at present, I have therefore detained him here. The enclosed letter will give your Excellency the names of the persons Dyckman is anxious should be brought off. I therefore request that your Excellency will take such measures for the purpose as you deem expedient."

The cautious import of this letter was that anyone who had associated with Arnold might be in the plot. But Arnold proved to have operated, like Macbeth, only with his wife. Samson's patriotism remained unsullied.

mean that the game could be carelessly played. An obvious cover-up would be a useless weapon of defense. And Drummond, who represented not Clinton but the Treasury, had his own career to attend to. Dyckman was faced with imperative new problems.

The Commissioners of Imprest had concerned themselves only with the past and had been separated by three thousand miles from the specific evidence that lay behind the accounts. But Major Drummond would deal with the present as well as the past, and was geographically perfectly placed for checking on wagons and horses and drivers.

Since Dalrymple was in London on another mission from Clinton to Lord Germain, Dyckman undoubtedly interviewed him about the present state of the Department. Endlessly noisy and self-pitying and self-righteous, the flabby non-military general could not hide from so shrewd and well-informed a man that he had helped himself with a greed and lack of discretion that endangered the position of all the quartermasters, past and present. Furthermore, what Dalrymple had to report about Clinton's position with the government was not encouraging for those who might have to cling to him in a political tempest. Clinton's interest had sunk so low that his ultimatum that he would resign unless certain things were done was received by Germain with seeming pleasure.

All the more because of Dalrymple's excesses, a strong and experienced hand would be needed in New York lest the investigation prove, when all the cards had been played, a major strategic error. The interests of Dyckman's clients had held him in England. The new situation hurried him towards home. He sailed during June, 1782, after a stay in England of almost exactly three and a half years.

CHAPTER SIX

◈

A Military Court

As he prepared to sail for America, Dyckman concluded that he could make a profit out of his taste and elegance, and also from his long wanderings as a solitary observer of the appearance and manners of the upper classes. Erskine, ever generous with the fortune Dyckman was helping him keep, contributed £600. Lord Cathcart grudgingly added another £100.

America had always imported her luxuries from England. Although goods could not now penetrate into areas the Rebels controlled, in British-held New York City there was an accelerated demand because of the concentration of highborn foreigners, and because prosperous Loyalist inhabitants (particularly the ladies) yearned to impress the aristocrats who had so miraculously been showered around them. The merchants regularly trading to New York were merely businessmen; States considered himself a connoisseur of excellences. Who else could not only select what was in the very best taste of the most up-to-date fashions, but, as a recent arrival from London, exemplify in his own person the finest and latest in men's furnishings?

On the sloop *Two Friends*, Dyckman sent ten "light matted" trunks containing goods valued at £628.5.8. Included were £126.17.0. worth of shoes, the treasure being six dozen pairs of "neat satin and silk pumps buttoned," worth £112. One hundred and thirty-one pairs of various kinds of silk hose came to £83.6.0.

There were waistcoats by the dozen, forty-two pieces of linen, fourteen yards of "superior" scarlet cloth, and much else. Dyckman also sent to New York on another ship another cargo (invoice lost).

States, nervous about sailing an ocean infested with French warships and Rebel privateers, drafted a will. It provided that the merchandise should be sold in New York by Cairns and the proceeds invested in England by Sherriff, the interest to go to his mother and after her death to be "equally divided" among Dyckman's three sisters. What he had on leaving New York asked Cairns to devote mostly to the use of Catalina — his salary and the proceeds of his share in the sloop *Matty* — was to be invested in America and the interest paid to "Eleanor Brewer now or late of New York, during the minority of her son States Brewer, now about two years old to whom I am godfather, and if he attains to the age of twenty-one years, I give the said monies to the said States Brewer for his use forever, but if he should die a minor, I give and bequeath the same to" (here, States, unable for the moment to determine a suitable legatee, left a blank).

Apart from the ungodson-like provisions for States Brewer, this draft is remarkable because States had entirely disinherited Catalina during their mother's lifetime. The beloved sister must in some serious way have offended her doting brother.

On his arrival in New York during July, 1781, Dyckman began a hasty correlating of the accounts he had submitted in London with the documents in the American office. Clinton soon appointed to investigate the quartermasters a board of officers presided over by the military governor of New York, General James Robertson who, according to the Tory observer Smith, had proved himself, in various offices he had held, a "jack-of-all-trades in the money-making way." There are indications in the Dyckman Papers that Robertson shared in the earnings of the wagon train. Another member of the Board was Cathcart's father-in-law, Andrew Elliot of the itching palm.

To get behind the vouchers, the board ordered a muster of all the wagons and drivers then in service. They were to appear at various locations at a date which, as far as the records reveal, gave the Department only three days' notice. Dyckman and his colleagues had to match hundreds of wagons and drivers, thousands of horses, with the statistics and names on a multiplicity of lists. But even its worst critics never accused the Department of inefficiency, and they were not playing to an exigent audience.

Any muster master who truly mustered would have torn the British military establishment from bottom to top. It was, for instance, standard practice to have in every regiment dummy soldiers for whom rations were allowed. The value of these rations was divided according to accepted formula, some of the proceeds going to the officers of the regiments, including honorary colonels, and some rising to the very top of the War Office in London.

The muster masters reported no irregularities in any of the musters.

Statistics collected by the investigator, Major Drummond, revealed what could not be hidden: the quartermasters' expenses Clinton had approved, were half again more than those approved by his predecessor, Howe.* This was the more remarkable because the army under Howe had been both larger and more active. In the absence of Dalrymple, who was still representing Clinton in London, deputy quartermasters Archibald Robertson and Henry Bruen undertook the defense. They testified that a principal explanation was the growing inveteracy of the inhabitants which increasingly forced up the cost of procuring teams.

---

*The figures reveal that Clinton had been assigned seven large wagons, each drawn by four horses, while his rival, Cornwallis, was allowed only three.

Although Cornwallis was hardly mentioned in the proceedings, Drummond made the main issue of the investigation the one Cornwallis had raised: whether the government could save large sums by purchasing rather than hiring the wagon train. Since the accounts which the law required gave no hints concerning the original costs of the horses and wagons, Drummond could only postulate figures that seemed reasonable. On this basis, he concluded that if the government bought the train, cost could be cut by two thirds.

Bruen and Robertson replied that they had (as they put it coyly) "received from the proprietors" information concerning the cost of purchase and repair which demonstrated that the present system was by far "the most effectual and economical." Drummond had overlooked so many expenses! He had not taken into consideration the cost of replacing horses lost by "glanders, farcy, staggers, etc., and the several casualties attending the train of an army which amounted to one third a year," etc., etc. Furthermore, "if the contractors had no indulgence in some particulars, it would not be worth their while to undertake so arduous a business, or to run the risk of so great a sum of money." But in case the government should decide to buy, "we are authorized to say that the greater proportion of the contractors will be glad to dispose of their property at a fair and reasonable valuation." It would not take, as Drummond had stated, only a few months' cost of hire to meet the purchase price, but "seven years, seven months, exclusive of interest and exchange on the principal sum advanced." Bruen and Robertson added, "We find ourselves extremely hurt by the innuendoes Drummond has thrown out."

Drummond reiterated that he was engaged in the investigation only because of "repeated orders from the Treasury." He assured Bruen and Robertson that nothing could be more repugnant to his feelings than hurting theirs.

The fiction perpetuated in the method of accounting that each team belonged to its driver had not even been given lip service in this investigation. It was assumed that fleets of teams were the property of investors. Yet Drummond, like Cornwallis before him, had not even hinted at what everyone in the know certainly knew: the proprietors and the quartermasters were one. The omission was so conspicuous that Drummond decided to make the army board shoulder the responsibility. It might be necessary, he suggested, to examine the actual contracts between the quartermasters and the proprietors to determine whether there existed "a fair and equitable bargain." Despite the devastating sound of this possibility, there was no need for Dyckman or anyone else to worry. The suggestion was automatically ignored.

Once more stating that he was only doing his duty and that he was not an expert on the subject, Drummond presented a new estimate, lower than before, of what "might possibly" be saved by not hiring but owning the wagons. One item postulated that various employees of the Department, including clerks like Dyckman, were really not in the service of the Crown but, although paid by the Crown, in the service of the proprietors.

The time had come when Drummond's figures needed to be refuted in greater detail than either Bruen or Robertson possessed. They presented to the board a paper which they stated had been prepared by "a gentleman conversant with the business." There can be little doubt that the anonymous individual was Dyckman. He was considered too low in rank to testify himself, or even to be mentioned by name. If this exclusion brought a pang to the yeoman's son from the Hudson Valley, he suppressed the feeling. Was he not enjoying and greatly profiting from the role he was assigned to play?

Whether or not the holes that Dyckman pricked in Drummond's estimates were taken at face value, they did make clear that to reach any solid results the probe would have to dig deeper than anyone wanted it to go. The board decided to give up. They showed sympathy for Drummond by not insisting that he back down formally. The board notified Clinton of his private admission that "his examination of so complicated a subject" had "not been perfectly exact," and that some circumstances (unspecified) had changed. "He thought it his duty to save the court from being involved in calculations or overwhelmed with treatises on a measure which . . . the abovementioned circumstances may have rendered improper." Adding that questions concerning the progressive increases of quartermaster costs were too complicated for an immediate decision, the board adjourned on December 1, 1781.

Dyckman had cause for self-congratulation. The triumphant muster had been impressive for refuting English suspicions that figures presented in the accounts were moonshine. And to get by without any censure is a favorable step even if the judges express themselves as puzzled.

In a separate development the issue of purchase rather than hire seemed to have been swept into the dustbin. During the investigation, word had come in that Cornwallis had surrendered himself and his army to a combined French and Rebel force at Yorktown. However bad for the British cause, this seemed to be fortunate for the quartermasters. Surely the defeated general had been so discredited that his ideas on military reform could be scoffed at!

It could not be foreseen that Cornwallis, driven by a desperate need to move the onus of military failure to the shoulders of his commander, would carry his feud with Clinton to ever greater heights. Since the quarrel came to involve the momentous question of who was most responsible for the military loss of the American colonies, it became in London a major concern of governmental and public attention. And with this flaming issue the matter of the quartermasters' accounts was to remain so entangled that it was not to be quieted for more than twenty years.

Yorktown was in itself a less serious defeat than Burgoyne's surrender of 1777. The British forces in America still outnumbered Washington's army by two to one, and the French fleet which had played the determining role in the debacle had sailed away, perhaps never to return. Yet the war had been going so badly for the British — after six years of expensive fighting the Rebels were as intransigent as ever — that the psychological effect of the surrender was tremendous. It was too soon actually to know how the British government would react, but word came through the lines that the Rebels were jubilant: they considered the war as good as over, their independence as good as won.

In the British military circles States often frequented, the reaction was mixed. No soldier likes to have been engaged in a losing war, but the officers were dreadfully bored. Those stationed in New York had smelt hardly any gunpowder in the three years since the Battle of Monmouth (June, 1778). They gambled for high stakes among themselves; engaged in amateur theatricals; seduced lesser Loyalist girls and common soldiers' wives — but the metropolitan diversions offered by New York City were contemptible when compared with London. And the Rebel guerrillas so hemmed the British in so that almost no country enjoyments were available. The officers yawned in the faces of Tories like Dyckman, expressing disgust for America and eagerness to go home.

In New York as in London, States felt most congenial with his fellow Americans. As a group, his compatriots, facing impoverished exile should the British abandon the war, were reacting like cornered animals. The optimistically named "Associated Loyalists" had been reinforced by the pitifully named "Board of Refugees." The two groups combined on hysterical violence. During a guerrilla raid on New Jersey, one of their number, Philip White, had been killed, and they had captured a militia captain, Joshua Huddy. Huddy was taken out of a prison ship, and hanged between the lines with placards on his breast. "Up

goes Huddy for Philip White," said one, and another expressed
determination to "hang man for man as long as a refugee is left
existing." His old friend Abraham Cuyler argued to Dyckman
that the reprisal was justified considering the nature of "the cause
and that numbers of Loyalists have been massacred by the
Rebels and not accounted for."

But Dyckman had no personal need for violent emotions.
Should the British give up, his close relatives, being all Rebels,
would profit. He himself would in any case return to London,
where he was well placed and had been living happily. True, he
had never intended to settle permanently in England, but there
were worse fates, and in a few years, when the rancor of war had
subsided, Americans who had served the British would probably
be allowed to come home.

During the winters, England vanished as if to another planet.
Every type of communication between Europe and North
America — men, goods, news — moved exclusively on square-
rigged sailing ships that did not attempt to cross some three
thousand miles of winter ocean. States could receive no information from London and in any case, even if he discovered that he
was desperately needed in London because the more lethal investigation threatened there had got under way, there was no way
of getting back to London. He used some of the time copying
out the accounts of the stores sent to America when Erskine was
quartermaster — more than a hundred thousand pounds'
worth — records that were to prove of great use in later investigations.

In New York City, States enjoyed a more agreeable worldly
position than he had ever before known. There existed here, it is
true, echoes of the British wealth and aristocracy which had so
clearly been far above him in London, but these individuals,
who callously extended their pleasure grounds out over the graves
in Trinity churchyard, were not integral to the environment. In-

stead of being looked up to, they were resented, even hated* by
the Loyalists with whom States associated. Where he had once
been scorned as the son of a broken innkeeper, States stood out
among his companions as a rich man of fashion.

Dyckman could well have realized 100 percent on the more
than £600 worth of goods he had brought from London. For his
services in connection with the recent investigation he had received £1,060, which shows how valuable those services were
considered. Cairns, who had been handling his affairs in America,
handed over a considerable surplus. On November 8, Dyckman
sent to London for investment £515: "I should prefer five or even
four percent with safety to a higher interest rate attended with a
larger risk." On December 5, he sent a second sum. That he had
to introduce himself to the broker as "a friend of Sir William
Erskine" suggests that this was the first of Dyckman's many at-
tempts to save money.

There was much left over. Since generosity was an essential
part of his character, we may assume that impoverished Loyalist
friends found him compliant. Although getting funds through
the lines was not easy, he managed to help his family. We know
that he met his brother Samson at Elizabethtown, New Jersey — probably by accompanying a flag of truce — and lent him
£100. Women's activities were in those days subject to little
supervision: Catalina reappeared in New York. States met her
bills, although not as lavishly as formerly. He became friendly
enough with a Mrs. Boxley for an invitation to say that he might
bring her if he pleased. He bought for £18.0.0. the furnishings
for a bed: a hair mattress, a white cotton counterpane, curtains, a
carpet, yards and yards of binding and fringe.

When the fine clothes Dyckman had brought with him from

---

*It could be argued that the English lost America not so much on any battlefield as in
occupied New York, to which leading Loyalists from all over the continent fled only to
be subjected to a more tyrannical military government than the Rebels had, in their most
violent anti-British propaganda, ever envisioned.

London lost their novelty and sheen, States had ample recourse to Hercules Mulligan, the tailor who is best known to history for having been somewhat in loco parentis to Alexander Hamilton when the youth had appeared in New York from the West Indies in the 1760's. States had been in New York for some six months when on November 10 he decided that one of his coats needed refacing. On December 4, he acquired a new double-breasted coat and buttons for a vest. Six days later, he needed a vest faced with silk twist, some breeches, and another vest of pure silk. Seven days after that, another tailor ran up a coat of light-colored cloth, a vest, and breeches. In another two days, he was back with Mulligan, for a vest and breeches. Six more days, and a pair of breeches with silk twist on the buttons. Three more days, a satin vest.

This seems to have completed his winter wardrobe. In the early months of 1782, his recorded purchases were mostly of accessories, some, like the pair of silk stockings (£1.4.0.), "for Miss Dyckman." There were pairs of buckles, many gloves, riding whips, scented powder, pomatum and lavender water, a red leather trunk and another trunk. The final purchase, "one lady's pocket book" (£3.4.0.) was obviously a farewell gift.

When in May the weather had ameliorated and Dyckman prepared to sail, he was inundated with requests from Loyalists who were sending or had sent sons to England. Would he "set" William Seton's son "down at his grandmother's . . . who lives at a home called the College House at Chidwick, directly back of Turnham Green"? Would be call on Abraham Cuyler's son "at Hackney, and let me know your opinion respecting his improvement"? Although a bachelor, States had a strong family sense. As subsequent letters of thanks demonstrate, he carried out such tasks meticulously.

CHAPTER SEVEN

✑

A Parliamentary Commission

DYCKMAN seems to have dawdled relaxedly in New York until ships arriving from London brought news that the dreaded investigation by the Parliamentary Commissioners Appointed to Examine, Take, and State the Public Accounts of the Kingdom had begun. After his own voyage the other way across the ocean, Dyckman reached London early in July, 1782. What was officially labeled *The Seventh Report* of the Commissioners had been signed just a month before. Dyckman's clients had surely secured a copy. They greeted him with black faces.

All that Dyckman had already achieved had been scorned by the Commissioners. They stated that it had been utterly impossible for the Auditors of Imprest, who had passed the accounts of Erskine, Sherriff and Cathcart, to reach reliable conclusions since the evidence could be checked only in America. "Numberless and in a variety of ways," commented the Commissioners, "may have been the frauds and impositions committed on the government."

The Commissioners urged that Parliament set up "an examination in North America by persons intelligent in the subject matter and unconnected with the expenditure." This, as Clinton was loudly to complain, utterly ignored the recent investigation in New York. If the report had reached the Commissioners across the winter seas, they must have ruled that Clinton and his board of officers were far from "unconnected with the expenditure."

[73]

The Commissioners had not, like the board in New York, tacked around the question of whether the quartermasters themselves were the proprietors of the wagon train. They sprang the question during an interrogation of Sherriff. The deputy quartermaster, who had been States's original employer, implied that the practice had not been initiated until he himself had been superseded as the head of the department by General Erskine. He stated as vaguely as he dared: "After the year 1776, he believed, several persons in the department of the quartermaster were the proprietors of some of the wagons and let them to the government at a set price."

The cat being out of the bag, Sherriff's fellow defendants were, in their subsequent testimony, less evasive. Erskine stated, "Many of the wagons and horses were the property of officers in the different departments, and he believes that the driver received at the office his own hire only and not that of the wagons and horses, which was paid to the proprietor." Erskine also vouchsafed the information that sometimes one person, deputized by the proprietors, signed to the receipts the names of the drivers. Cathcart was the most specific about the ownership: "Upon inquiry, he found that the wagons and horses were in general the property of a few officers who either were or had been in this department."

The Commissioners' comment was violent. The duty of quartermasters was to check and control contractors. The defense Dyckman's clients had presented, that the prices charged and paid had been established by the commander in chief, was invalid, since the quartermasters' trust dictated securing, whenever possible, a lower price. The diatribe went on to include the statement that it was to the interest of the proprietors to see to it that the wagons were captured or destroyed by the enemy so that they could get the extra profit.

"In such a contest between duty and interest, it is not uncharitable to suppose that the public interest will frequently be sacrificed to private emolument. But this is not the only mischief: this practice has a danger to corrupt and endanger the service of the army; it weakens the military discipline; it infuses into the soldier the thirst for gain; and diverts his attention from honor and the country's service to the pursuit of wealth, and that too by entrenching upon the treasure of his country."

Having thus struck a noble stance, the Commissioners acknowledged the realities of the situation: men of birth and power, paid tiny salaries, administered tremendous sums in the realization that they would be required personally to reimburse the government for any irregularities. Obviously, "these officers would hardly have engaged in business of this kind without the expectation of some advantage." The Commissioners were thus "led to endeavor to form a judgment on the probable advantages" of the quartermasters.

Official statistics stated that the hire of a wagon, driver, and four horses was £219 a year. Drivers were paid a shilling twopence a day, which reduced the amount earned by the owner to £197.4.4. "Repairs for the wagons and harness and food of the drivers and horses being found by the public," these did not need to be included in the calculation.

The next essential step was to determine what was not officially available: the original cost to the proprietors. Being "cautious that our examination did not lead to self-accusation," the Commissioners did not try to elicit from the quartermasters what they had paid for the wagons and horses. Like Major Drummond in New York, they made their own estimates. But while Drummond had been reduced to almost pure guesswork, the Commissioners had recourse to an authority whom they did not name but whose identity was obvious in the total context: Cornwallis had been released by the Rebels on parole.

Computed at "the highest price," so the Commissioners announced, a four-horse wagon would cost £20 and each horse £15. This meant that the proprietor would recover his purchase money in three months. Then, if he possessed fifty large wagons and two hundred horses, a proprietor would receive £9,885.8.4. a year, without capital investment and "secure of all risk." Had Cornwallis's system been applied during the period under examination, the government would have been saved £241,690. Cornwallis's system "should be put in force at once throughout the army."

Cornwallis backed up in personal testimony the implication that Clinton was grievously at fault. Still in command in America, Clinton could not be present to defend himself. Nor was any opportunity given Dyckman's clients to rebut Cornwallis's figures.

In summing up, the Commissioners produced another burst of righteousness — no officer "ought to be permitted to carve out for himself an interest in the public trust!" — but the paragraph went on to acknowledge that "if the interest had been productive," it remained a question "how far such profit belongs to the public." Parliament should rule on this and also decide "whether by bills of discovery filed by the proper officer of the Crown or any other means," an effort be made to force from the quartermasters their personal accounts as proprietors.

The report of his army board which Clinton had sent to the Treasury disappeared into a box, but the *Seventh Report* was printed up in an elegant format to be (as Clinton complained) "very well received by the public." Although Dyckman undoubtedly shared the dismay of the rest of the Department, the *Seventh Report* was to prove for him a stroke of good fortune. Had Cornwallis and the Commissioners not intervened; had the remaining quartermasters' accounts passed the auditors as smoothly as those he had already presented; and had they all then lain quiet, the need for Dyckman's services would soon have come to an end. Had the *Report* actually, as some of its passages threatened, blown his clients from the water, not only would his employment have ceased, but he might have been caught in the explosion. A society dependent on its own prerogatives was not averse to setting up less well-born functionaries as scapegoats for popular wrath.

As it was, the *Seventh Report* continued for decades to walk, like an accusing ghost, at the feasts of the Department, yet it carried no effective weapon. The public disclosure that the Department owned the wagon train was embarrassing, but could not have come as a surprise to sophisticated individuals who knew how the world wagged. The recommendation of staging a new rigorous investigation on American soil changed from an improbability to an impossibility as the British occupation of New York moved towards complete withdrawal. And the Commissioners' passionate praises of Cornwallis tainted the report with the odor of propaganda in the war against Clinton. The political tenor of the investigation was underlined by the final reference of the basic issues to decisions by Parliament.

The Commissioners had responded with no indignation to Erskine's acknowledgment that his duties in the field had prevented him from knowing any more than appeared on the face of the vouchers. The Commissioners had without comment interviewed Dalrymple in London, far separated from his duties in New York. It was thus accepted that the top officials were appointed for other reasons than attendance to the functions of their offices. The chariness of the Commissioners lest they dig too deep, their recommendation that Parliament should determine whether "interest" had resulted not in profit but in too much profit, revealed that, for all the perorations on military honor, it was not the practices themselves that were under attack but how and by whom they were applied.

The issue was fundamentally whether the individuals on too "slender appointments" had in too short a time taken too much. Here was a flock of variables. How strong was the dynastic and political clout of the men under suspicion? The answer to this question did much to determine what was a slender appointment, how short was too short a time, and when the profit became unsuitably great.

As in all structured societies, form was considered of the greatest importance; appearance had to be impeccable. The two investigations, that in New York and that in London, however they otherwise differed, were equally concerned with determining whether procedures had been carried through exactly according to rule. And the Commissioners might have been promulgating an advertisement for the importance to his employers of Dyckman's handling of the accounts when they stated, "Could a single instance of fraud be discovered, such a discovery would so vitiate and corrupt that account as to subject the whole to revision and unravelment, although adjusted and passed with all the solemnity of the Exchequer."

CHAPTER EIGHT

✑

The Exile Yearns for Home

THE continuing investigations of the quartermasters were
by no means continuous. While documents lingered for
months in pigeonholes and then emerged to languish on
desks, Dyckman's responsibilities halted. He was being too well
paid to seek other gainful employment. Although he had to stay
within range of a call, he had plenty of free time in which to
amuse himself.

Dyckman had overcome the feelings of strangeness and
wonder that had made him, during his first stay in England,
spend so many hours haunting inconspicuously the gathering
places of aristocrats, admiring particularly the fine ladies. He described himself still as "a great wanderer," and was inclined to
travel by himself, but he had become highly convivial in the
reasonably well-off circles where he was naturally at home. He
would, he wrote, happily make a detour of a hundred miles to
see a friend, but he was often delayed in the road by acquaintances proffering hospitality. Once arrived at his destination, he
would fall in with whatever was going on, even joining a cheerful group at pitching hay. He was considered a master at talking
"on the soft subject," to young ladies, so much so that other
swains had, as a friend wrote, "very little chance against your
Lordship." Another companion commented on States's fondness
for "retirement and sentimental walks." He was not considered
"so much a man of business" as to neglect a friend.

[79]

"Write me a long letter," an absent companion begged, "and tell me a number of little incidents which you suppose would have occasioned a laugh at a tête-à-tête. What new wonders are displayed this season in great world of London and Westminster? Has the learned pig walked off the stage, and which of the creations has succeeded him? Apropos of the stage — but shall I mention the admirable Mrs. Siddons? I can never mention her without feeling my heart strings vibrate. Tell me all about her. Send me any little matter that strikes your attention — even advertisements, handbills, songs, etc. As I converse with ladies, think of them too."

There can be no doubt that he was generally considered a most charming man. His generosity was warm. He lent a companion the large sum of £750 as an accommodation not carrying interest. When another friend asked for £10 so that he could travel to Scotland, not as he could afford but "in a manner I could wish," Dyckman sent him £12.

States did not cease to be impressed by English sophistication. He found his justification and self-expression in the mimicking of the tastes he saw around him. But his imitation was typical of the Loyalists by being singularly unfruitful.

There were other Americans in London who were much concerned with the glories of European culture, but they were not Loyalists. Most conspicuous was the painter Benjamin West whom States's client, Lord Cathcart, had tried to expel from the court of George III because of his admitted sympathy with the Rebels. West, and the "American School" of painters around him,* applied the originality and drive that had set off the fight in America to revolutionize aspects of European art. Grasping

---

*West's colleague, John Singleton Copley, has been called a Loyalist but he actually was a neutral who, by trying to keep peace in Boston, got involved in situations he could not bear. After George III had acknowledged American independence, Copley painted into a portrait what was probably the first American flag to be hoisted in England. When, after many years in London, he considered sailing back to America, he was warned that he had become "too rank a Jacobin" to be acceptable in Federalist Boston.

the "grand style" of painting (towards which the portraitist Sir Joshua Reynolds vainly yearned) they created explosion after explosion: bringing neo-classicism up to date by depicting heroes in modern costume; fighting the Church of England taboo against religious art; anticipating the romantic movement by finding grandeur in the Middle Ages and in modern times. They depicted the gruesome and the horrible within a style that had been dedicated to what was nobly elevated. The impression they made was to remain active, in Paris as elsewhere in Europe, for a half century.

Dyckman would not have been a Loyalist had he shared such revolutionary instincts. He shied away from esthetic innovation. His object was to purchase what is "new and much admired here." By this phrase he meant what was most recently in fashion among the socially correct. If he could not talk as an equal with the fashionable beauties or even gain access to their drawing rooms, he could love and possess what they possessed. He kept as happy records the bills for what he expensively bought — bills by the score bearing the letterheads of well-established merchants.

But all was not serene. A routine bill for goods bought in 1785 included charges more frightening for the future than anyone could realize. In February and again in April, Dyckman bought "gouty shoes."

Dyckman was later to assert that he had so impressed the officials with whom he was negotiating that he had been invited to join them. He was offered a post in the auditor's office which could become worth the large sum of £500 a year. He would have been given a lifetime career in England, respectable and subterraneanly powerful. When trying to use his refusal as a crowbar to pry money from Sir William's son, he insisted that he had been motivated by his realization that "the stability of Erskine's fortune depended on his services." This was surely a consideration, for States felt his obligations to his patrons, but it seems clear that he was not really tempted to change from the New World to the Old.

As the experiences of Loyalist refugees went, Dyckman had been highly privileged in his contacts with the British. Not beggared or pushed around, he had from the start been taken into a flourishing official enterprise. He had been treated kindly and handsomely rewarded. He had lived well and made friends. Yet he found that the nation which he had believed would be the same as America but better, automatically superior wherever there was a deviation, was in some deep way alien to him. His brief return to New York in 1781 and 1782 had unsettled him. As he became more familiar with "the mother country," he felt less and less a birthright member of the British family. He yearned to get back to the place where he had been born.

Dyckman did not intend to settle down in New York City and wrestle with the patricians who would, whichever way the war turned out, surely take precedence there. Nor did he intend to use his sophistication learned in London to reform what, despite his homesickness, he still considered the crudeness of native American society. (Had he yearned to be a leader, the life here being described would have been very different.) He had not yet been driven by the need to drown desperate tribulations into planning a great house that would rival the mansions of the great families of the Hudson River valley. His ambition was to achieve what his father had failed to achieve. He would return to the family enclave, now in Westchester County, and stand out among his neighbors. That the Dyckmans had not raised their sights high is revealed when States witnessed, after his return to New York, the indenture of one of his nephews to a saddler. From London, States wrote Samson to buy against his return a "small" farm in the neighborhood. Here he would retire, living comfortably and securely on what he had earned, proudly showing his possessions to the yeomen who lived around him.

Whether or not Dyckman would achieve resettlement in America involved happenings on both sides of the ocean, but whatever calls might be made on him in England, the developments least under his own control were those in America. If Great Britain managed to reestablish sovereignty over the colonies — or, at least, the colony of New York — there would be no problem. But if New York became part of an independent nation, his situation as a Loyalist who had joined the British would be at best complicated, at worst hopeless. He might never be allowed to set foot again on American soil.

Dyckman was hardly back in England after his stay in New York when he received bad news in a letter from Cuyler: "To all appearances, the Rebel rulers reject any offer of peace short of independence . . . . a circumstance not unexpected by you that is acquainted with the temper of the Rebel demigods."

A month later, Cuyler wrote, "Since the arrival of the June packet, we have been in the utmost consternation on the unaccountable steps taken by the [English] administration to propose the independence of the country in the first instance towards a general peace." Some American Loyalists nurtured a hope that the proposal would not be ratified by Parliament, "yet we must remain until the next arrival in the most disagreeable suspense." If British sovereignty were "given up, you may well suppose here will be no safety, and in that case numbers of Loyalists must be set afloat, for no stipulation in their favor will be complied with. I cannot describe to you my feelings. . . . I shall with numbers of Loyalists remove to Canada. . . . If this country should be relinquished, direct for me at Quebec to the care of Major Holland."

But even now, when all seemed lost, Cuyler could not believe that the Loyalists were among Americans a minority: "By late accounts, a far greater part of the country would prefer a reconciliation with dependence to independence."

Did Dyckman consider it possible, another Tory correspondent asked, "that it should be determined by our [royal] court to evacuate our hosts from America? I have so firm a reliance in the justice and humanity of His Majesty that it appears to me *impossible*."

After the Provisional Peace Treaty, which acknowledged independence, had been signed, States received an outburst from one of the men with whom he had clinked glasses at Albany in that fateful toast to the King eight years before. "The fatal moment . . . ," wrote Benjamin Hilton, "has at last arrived. We are all undone and ruined even beyond hope. May the execrable managers of this inglorious peace be ever execrated by their God and country! Thousands have emigrated and thousands are still to emigrate to Nova Scotia."

This was tragic news, but most of the Tories who fled were either the most conspicuous or the most apprehensive. It was the fate of those who were trying to make their way in America that riveted the attention of Dyckman and the run of the refugees in London. Dyckman had not borne arms against the patriots nor did he menace anyone by having had property that he might wish to get back, which had been confiscated and was now being enjoyed by a Rebel. As far as American officialdom knew, he had done no more than merely achieve necessary support by working as a clerk in a British military department. Most of the other Americans in London had, during their long exile, proceeded even more obscurely. The fates of ordinary Loyalists in America would prophesy their own futures. It is both surprising (and revealing) how few of those who had fled America out of loyalty to the Crown did not now yearn to go home. This is one of the many phenomena indicating that the American Revolution was caused less by oppressive laws passed in England than a fundamental dichotomy which had evolved between the two societies.

In the more-than-ever alien streets of London, the Loyalists' ears were ever cocked for news. Silence alternated with the bursts of information that came after ships from New York had docked: hundreds of private letters; newspapers; travelers, often refugees, subject to cross-examination. Unlike the many drifters whose address was the New York Coffee House, Dyckman received his letters at George Street. But, of course, he hurried to the coffee house to find out what the others had learned. There was not only swapping of information but endless discussion to extract from reports often contradictory what it all portended.

Although the war had in essence been terminated by the Provisional Treaty, the British still occupied New York, awaiting word of the Definitive Treaty. Loyalist refugees, eager to resettle in the regions from which they had fled, were flocking through the relaxed military lines. Thus were started the multitudinous whirlpools of confusion that were communicated to Dyckman and all the denizens of the New York Coffee House.

In the history books we read of laws passed and official policies laid down, but we are not told much concerning the spottiness of enforcement beyond the cases where rules could be routinely applied. Most refugees, anonymous in connection with major policy, returned to families more or less influential and more or less glad to repossess them, to old friends and enemies. And once arrived, they behaved in a variety of ways. Those were best off who merged inconspicuously with the countryside, were respectful to the political leaders who had exiled them, cast no covetous glances on their confiscated farms now occupied by patriots.

As nest eggs, many of the refugees brought with them such European merchandise as had been unprocurable for years in their native heaths. The goods were in such demand that the sellers, as they charged high prices, were able to insist on being paid in hard money. Outraged in any case by the competition, the established storekeepers insisted that traitors were monopolizing the little specie that loyal Americans had held onto to do business with. Although defeated on the battlefields, the Tories now flocked to the polls in such numbers that it seemed to fevered brains that they might grasp victory by determining elections. Wrath exploded, but it was neighborhood wrath, directed at some people and not others. Surely the repressive laws passed by the legislatures, although too lenient for the man down the road whom you distrusted, did not apply at all to your friend and cousin!

John Kortright, a captain in the British army whom States had lent £750 to buy a major's commission, belonged to a powerful New York trading family most of whom had been patriots. He sailed blithely from England to collect what he owed. From June to December, 1783, he wrote States enthusiastically. He was "greatly pleased with the country," and intended to stay. Since "I have no doubt but that everything will be as we wish," he expected to see Dyckman in New York during the spring. "Your brother has given me a very pleasing account of the farm he bought you."

Kortright's gleeful communications were interrupted by a letter from Hilton, dated July 2. "All the Loyalists who had gone out of New York," Hilton screamed, were "whipped and scourged and forced to return. . . . There is no asylum for us in any of the states. . . . Almost every town and precinct on the continent have formed themselves into committees and passed resolves the most harsh and inflammatory ag[ainst] the return of this deluded, deserted, and most unfortunate class of human beings. . . . All we have to hope for is that the madness and intoxication that pervades the whole continent, and the clashing of interests of the various states will be their ruin, and bring about a favorable revolution."

Although this was most depressing, other news in Hilton's letter cut closer to Dyckman's heart.

States already knew that his sister Caty had returned to Rebel territory. Now Hilton expressed concern lest Dyckman had heard from a Mr. J. Jones, who had sailed to London, the report that "your sister was dead, occasioned by a sore foot." Having expressed happiness "at being able to inform you . . . she is alive and well," Hilton continued, without any break in the sentence, to send States congratulations on his sister's marriage to "a Major Hale in the Continental service, who I am told stands fair in the world." So much having been communicated, Hilton switched to other matters.

Was this report of his sister's marriage any more believable than the denied rumor that she was dead? Surely his beloved Caty would never have taken such a step without consulting or at least informing him! Nor would the other members of the family have left him uninformed. There was no need to abandon hope.

Then there appeared in London his close associate Hugh Cairns, just arrived from New York. Cairns had been personally informed by Samson of Caty's marriage.

Prudently, States held himself in check for "a few days." Then he composed to Samson a masterpiece of control: "I neither expected nor wished to be consulted on the subject, or even to have notice whenever she meant to change her situation. The distance between us, and the probability that the person she would choose to entrust her happiness with would be a stranger to me, left me no right to expect it. But surely though it was unnecessary to inform me of her intention, I might reasonably have expected to have been made acquainted with the circumstance after it took place, in a more agreeable way than by report. I address myself to you particularly, because you were at New York not many days before Mr. Cairns left it. A few minutes would have been sufficient to have informed me of her husband's name and situation in life. Though I might not know him personally, you could have made me acquainted with his character, which I trust would have removed my fears for her happiness. I have too good an opinion of my sister to distress myself with any unreasonable apprehensions, for I cannot think but she both consulted and acted by the advice of her brothers." He was so well convinced of this "that I feel no more anxiety than is natural on such an occasion, no more than I should feel, did I know and approve her choice. If the prospect before her is a pleasing one, I will enjoy it with her, and I do not mean to cloud it with doubts and apprehensions. . . . As I am certain her silence proceeded from diffidence and modesty, I am far from being displeased with her." As for her not informing him "after it happened . . . she might well suppose you would not neglect what probably she so much wished. I trust you have taken the first opportunity after your return to New York to remove my anxiety by giving me every information on the subject. Give my affectionate love to my mother."

This communication tells us much concerning Dyckman's success as a negotiator. That he was given to turbulent emotions and that they were particularly involved with Caty, past and future events make very clear. Five years before, when he was first in England, his letters to Caty were frighteningly explicit. But now everything is covered with a mask of sweetness, of reasonableness, of charm. His upbraidings of his brother could hardly have been more gentle. He exonerated — even praised — Caty, by attributing her "silence" to "diffidence and modesty." Although it is clear that apprehensions remained, he assured Samson that he had calmed his apprehensions on the conviction that she had acted on the advice of her brothers. He did not (a resolve which he would have done well to keep) wish his "doubts and apprehensions" to cloud Caty's happiness.

There were those who suspected the sincerity of the agreeable and appreciative face States put before the world. "Why do you rally me," he asked in a letter to one friend, "on the civility of my speeches?" and he then wittily turned his defense into another compliment: surely it would have been folly for him to "offer anything but my real sentiments to one of your experienced, nice judgement."

Daniel Hale, Dyckman's new brother-in-law, the possessor (as the old usage went) of Caty, came on strong. States threw out the first page of what seems to have been Hale's first letter, keeping only the sheets that had to do with business. The scrap begins: "would be happy to hear from you what your prospects and determination for the future are, in which I cannot help feeling myself interested.

"Permit me to add a few words on the subject of the farm at King's Ferry. It was ever a fixed principle with me never to connect myself with a family until I was permanently fixed in a regular line of business that promised at least a genteel support. The times for the last seven years were such as prevented my being in such situation though I have at times had considerable property in my possession. Depreciation of money, misfortunes in trade, and probably some neglects have drained a great part of it out of my hands, and had I not fortunately secured a part in fast property, the whole might in different ways have slipped from me, as there was no possibility of investing it as a capital in a regular line of business from the turbulence of the times, in which case, I flatter myself, from the advantages I have had in being regularly bred in the store of a merchant formerly of some prominence in this city [Albany], I could have kept it together and improved it.

"The mutual affection which had for a long time subsisted between your sister and myself induced me to forgo my original determination and request her in marriage which was completed with the cheerful consent of all the family, her brother Sam in particular. I have since that, though heartily prejudiced against all copartnerships, been induced to accept the offers of a merchant of Albany of one half the profits of his business with a store completely started and by far the best stand in town. I have made part of my advance and must depend [for] the remainder, about £400," on the value of the farm States had "so generously" given Caty.

The new relation did not hesitate to inform States what his relations wanted him to do: the Dyckmans wanted him to purchase the farm. Hale wished he could "insist" otherwise. However, he would draw on States for the £400 in the spring unless States objected, "in which case no difficulty would induce me to do it." If States did not consider it "proper" to acquire the farm, "on your arrival in America, which I have no doubt will be the ensuing summer," Hale would, he promised, pay back the unsecured money.

The stranger who was yet so intimate a connection signed himself, "believe me, with sentiments of real affection, your friend and brother, Dan'l Hale."

With the coming of spring, Hale drew on Dyckman for £650, New York currency, which he announced included repairs to the house. Then he launched into an account of the political situation. The New York State legislature had passed a law providing that, among other classes of Loyalists, "those who have held offices of profit or honor during the war" were "defranchised." Furthermore, all those who had, as Dyckman had done, refused "to take certain oaths" were threatened with the penalties of treason. States was not mentioned in the act by name, "though I believe all your acquaintances are." The Council of Revision would probably confirm the law as a "political expedient" which "would satisfy the multitude" but "may again be removed." At a recent election, the "well disposed inhabitants" had installed some moderates, "and I am well convinced anything that may at present be unconstitutional or unjust . . . will soon be corrected."

Hale had been assured by a member of the legislature that "in his opinion the law could not affect anyone who came to the country as a visitor and not a resident to remain." Therefore, in Hale's opinion, States could come over that summer "without any risk." He could then determine the situation for himself. Caty had had a son who was "an uncommonly fine child," and the Hales hoped States would stay with them in Albany.

In March, 1785, John Kortright wrote States not to "think of returning except to share the many impositions your friends are daily experiencing." Those who had stayed within the British lines had been assessed a total of £100,000. In deciding whom to pounce on, the assessors had clearly used other considerations than ability to pay. Unable to satisfy the assessors, some of States's friends were having "their goods and furniture sold at public auction." Kortright was not personally affected and was staying on.

States's most distinguished companion in London was an erudite lawyer, Peter Van Schaack, who had codified the laws of the Colony of New York. He had played an important role as a patriot at the start of the Rebellion, but experience and further study had made him publicly recant. Officially banished, he appeared in England. States found Van Schaack so compelling that he considered leaving Mrs. Tait's to share lodgings with his distinguished friend, but the older man bowed out gracefully: "My imperfections are sufficiently troublesome to myself without making them so to others."

He discussed with States by the hour whether it was safe to go home. Van Schaack's information came from the conservative leaders in New York; he was an intimate of John Jay, who, as a peace commissioner, had tried to get effective protection for the Loyalists included in the treaties that acknowledged independence. Van Schaack quoted assurances he had received that it would be safe to return, but Dyckman could not be persuaded that what was applicable to a man with such friends as Jay would also be applicable to him. Van Schaack remembered that Dyckman had thought him "too sanguine, under the bias of an overwhelming partiality towards my countrymen."

Having made the plunge, Van Schaack wrote ecstatically from New York. "My most sanguine expectations have been answered both as to my reception and the state of the country. All is tranquility and a portion of liberality prevails here far beyond what would easily be believed in London, but I have no doubt that zealots would like to interrupt this state of things, and the intemperate conduct of individuals may give them a handle." Two months later he announced, "The distinction of Whig and Tory is no more." But Dyckman did not sail.

The Quartermaster Department was getting deeper and deeper into trouble. Dyckman's services were increasingly needed by his clients in London. And further service would add substantially to the funds which would enable the young man to retire for the rest of his life, preferably on the banks of the Hudson, in comfort, extravagance, and safety.

Dyckman, whose temperament sought tranquility, may well have been not unhappy to postpone confronting his beloved sister as the wife of the bossy, blowhard Hale. Although the prospect was made more alluring, it was also made more frightening by the fact that almost every letter he received from New York communicated the extreme eagerness of the married woman for her brother's return. In forwarding a letter (now destroyed) from Caty herself, Hale conceded that it revealed his wife's unhappiness at States's absence. Then the husband tried to make the situation more satisfactory to himself by referring to Dyckman's sister as "my little girl," and specifying that he had sent on the letter "in compliance to her wishes, which her kind and affectionate conduct to me so fully merits."

One of States's correspondents reported, "Her eyes overflowed when she spoke of you, or rather every time your name was mentioned."

∾

CHAPTER NINE

Explosions on the Long Road

THE *Seventh Report* of the Parliamentary Commissioners menaced the landscape like a distant thundercloud. However, the Lords of the Treasury did not take to their heels. Erskine's, Sherriff's, and Cathcart's accounts lay quietly in the Treasury files, although not so permanently buried that they could not be exhumed. The money was in the former quartermasters' hands. Gamblers all, they did not hesitate to spend it. But they were glad to have Dyckman standing by with his kit of lightning rods.

Clinton had been replaced as commander in chief in America by Guy Carleton, who had sat with the Commissioners of the *Seventh Report*. Carleton's quartermaster, the Brook Watson known to posterity because Copley painted him being attacked while swimming by a shark, was ordered to buy for the Crown the necessary wagons and horses. The three remaining high officials of the old Quartermaster Department — deputy quartermasters Henry Bruen and Archibald Robertson, Quartermaster General John Dalrymple — came to London. When they put their accounts in Dyckman's hands, he acquired a very mixed bag of new clients.

In all the accusations that down the years plagued the quartermasters, incompetence was never asserted. It was acknowledged that whenever there was a need for transport and it could possibly be supplied, it had been there. This efficiency was, of course, not the creation of the highborn quartermasters general, who directed their concern to matters more commensurate with their worldly station. The work was done by the deputy quartermasters general, among whom Bruen was the most active.

Henry Bruen's grandfather had been one of those hated soldiers of Cromwell's invading army who had stayed in Ireland. The family remained obscure until the grandson, in America as a captain in the Sixty-third Foot, revealed conspicuous efficiency that caught the eyes of the Quartermaster Department. No sooner did the quartermaster profits start cascading into Bruen's pockets than he began to demonstrate an obsessive urge to insert himself among the Irish gentry by establishing a huge landed estate. His first purchase was a gentleman's house in County Carlow, which he improved into a mansion. Buying from the Beauchamp, Grogan, and Waley families, he extended his domain beyond Carlow into County Wexford. When established aristocrats expressed, along with dismay, suspicions as to how the interloper had become so rich, Bruen reacted with outrage:

"I moved in a humble sphere, and took an active part as I had a great supply by land and water to furnish, which I did in the most efficacious manner. . . . I ventured a large capital in the undertaking and if by great risk and attention to labor, I have succeeded and acquired the reward that is due, I must, if attacked, appeal to the laws of Great Britain."

Bruen might cry about the laws of Great Britain, but he was one of those from whom the application of those laws was supposed to protect the nation: a man without dynastic or political prerogatives who, "on a slender appointment," had acquired what his unbridled expenditures revealed as tremendous funds. The other quartermasters viewed him angrily, since he was tainting their common cause. They were horrified by a rumor that he had spent £100,000 on a single purchase. For his part, Bruen accused the other quartermasters, particularly General

Dalrymple, of cheating him by not acknowledging sums he had lent them and by hiding proceeds in which he should have had a share. He cried loudly that he was slandered. He wrote darkly, "It is disagreeable to have your mail opened."

It was Bruen who had decided, when Dyckman had first sailed for London, to keep paying him his salary in New York. When not in a snobbish mood, Bruen and his wife circulated naturally with States and his friends. In England, Bruen was to reward States with conspicuous generosity and to fawn on him when begging his assistance. Yet Bruen complained that Dyckman "has for a long time been playing an odd game. In short, he thinks his services deserve a great deal more than he has received and therefore complains. I never looked upon him as more than a *clerk* entrusted with the common details of the office. . . . This man must be checked."

Although it took a little time for his difficulties to heat up, the investigators gave Bruen what Dyckman described as "an awful time."

The extent to which family, personality, and behavior influenced the investigations is revealed by the contrast between the treatment accorded to Bruen and Robertson. Stemming from an ancient Scottish family, Robertson was a first cousin of the famous architects, the Adam brothers. Himself a gifted amateur watercolorist (as several of the illustrations in this book show), he depicted the scenery of New York. Friendship with Sir William Erskine had brought him to the Department, where he carried out his duties as quietly as Bruen was noisy.

After the war, Robertson, like Bruen, used his quartermaster money to create a landed estate. However, the house he bought in Perthshire and greatly enlarged had belonged to his ancestors. He gradually acquired thirty-five thousand acres in ways that did not annoy his neighbors. Rather than being hounded, he attracted more prerogative. When England was girding in 1798 for defense against a threatened Napoleonic invasion, Robertson was appointed commander of a regiment of Perthshire volunteers. "Fortune," he commented good-naturedly, "sometimes flows upon a man. . . . You know, this must be a profitable concern. No matter. It is offered in so handsome a manner by the Lord Lieutenant and the gentlemen concerned that I cannot get off, though my profits should come very smartly over the left shoulder. These are not times when a man should be too scrupulous. I am heartily in the cause and will stick to it." He added, "I only wish I had the use of my legs."

General Dalrymple came from one of the most conspicuous and most hated Scottish families. He carried with him an ancestral curse.

The Dalrymples' seat was Wigtown, at the extreme southeast of Scotland. The family was denounced in 1906 by a local historian as "new settlers in the district" because Sir Hugh Dalrymple of Stair, a lawyer, had taken advantage of the "troubles" of some old families to secure their lands "for himself." The date of this invasion was 1371. The outrage might eventually have been forgiven had it not been for the "extraordinary" activity of the Dalrymples across the border in England which, so the historian commented sourly, "gave insight into" the new road to success in the adoption of "law as a profession."

James Dalrymple, a descendant of Hugh, became an important judge under Cromwell but conspired with General Monk to procure the restoration of Charles II. He was rewarded.

The Stuarts were accused in Scotland of deserting their people to revel in the greater prestige and wealth of the English crown. Sir Walter Scott vociferously complained that they administered what should have been their homeland through such venal deputies as James Dalrymple. The second chapter of Scott's *Bride of Lammermoor* gives an horrendous picture of how the upstart lawyer (there called Sir William Ashton), hating the true Scottish aristocrats because they made him feel inferior, stole their lands by shyster legal tricks, and used his office to suppress their religion and imprison their bodies.*

It was believed in Scotland that James Dalrymple was dominated by his wife and that she was a witch. Prudently concerned for the continuing prosperity of her family, she included with her own soul, in her contract with the devil, the souls of all her descendants. The smell of brimstone continued, indeed, to hover over the Dalrymples. The misfortune of the witch's daughter, who went mad on her wedding night, became the theme of Scott's novel, and is reenacted at every performance of the Donizetti opera, *Lucia di Lammermoor.* Another daughter was believed a witch in her own right, and one grandson killed another.

When James Dalrymple was in his seventies and his son John had taken over the deputized rule of Scotland, the astute lawyers played an active part in exiling the increasingly unpopular James II to bring in William and Mary. The new king created James Dalrymple Viscount Stair and continued John as virtual ruler of Scotland.

John Dalrymple, who is quoted as exulting that the "thieving" Catholic highlanders could all be exterminated "in the long, cold nights," was held responsible for one of the English outrages that still makes Scottish blood run hot: the Massacre of Glencoe (1692) during which royal troops made a partially successful effort to kill all the males of the MacDonald clan. For nine years thereafter, Dalrymple was unable to show his face in Parliament, but in another three years Queen Anne — the influence went on to still another monarch — created him Earl of Stair. In 1707, he signed for Scotland a treaty of union with England which earned for the new Earl in his home country "the memorable sobriquet" of "The Curse of Scotland."

John's son, John, the second Earl of Stair, became major gen-

---

*The picture was so recognizable that Scott found it necessary to deny that Dalrymple had been his model.

eral under Marlborough and a major diplomat representing George I to Louis XIV. Depleting his fortune through lavish, if patriotic, entertaining in Paris, "he tried," so reports the *Dictionary of National Biography*, "to repair it by stockjobbing on a large scale." After that, as his political power rose and fell, he spent much time on the family Wigtown estate, in the village of Inch bordering the estuary of that name, where he laid out the famous gardens that are still a tourist attraction. He also developed the breed of horses known as Galloways. A disreputable anecdote about him was immortalized by Scott in his novel *Chronicles of Cannongate*. Wishing to force a rich widow to marry him, he bribed her servants to let him sneak into the room where she was known to say her morning prayers. By exhibiting himself half-dressed in the window over Edinburgh's High Street, he so compromised the widow that she had no choice but marry him.

The quartermaster's father, John Dalrymple, fifth Earl of Stair, had, as a member of Parliament, opposed the measures that led to the American Revolution. After he had lost his seat, he became known as "The Cassandra of the State" because of his pamphlets which prophesied that governmental improvidence would bankrupt England. He insulted his successors in Parliament by stating that "at the nod of their managers [they] vote away the millions of their country that is now nicknamed free." His son's role as quartermaster did not keep the fifth Earl from excoriating, towards the end of the Revolution, the cost of the extraordinary military services.

Who could resist the temptation to avenge Cassandra's insults on his invitingly vulnerable son? Whether or not anyone believed that the ancient family compact with the devil extended to the former quartermaster, the opinion was certainly alive that "disagreeable matters" were usually "mixed up with the prosperity of the Dalrymples."

McKerlie, the anti-Dalrymple chronicler of Galloway, wrote

that Dyckman's client was "described as humpbacked [the utterly unmilitary general may well have been round-shouldered] and a great spinner of the reel [one who glibly rattled off songs and stories]." A boyhood portrait shows him with thin, sensitive face; a later caricature as monstrously fat. The picture of him that emerges from the Dyckman papers is apprehensive in a manner that would be appealing in a small boy, jumpy, indecisive, self-pitying, shifty, and greedy.

After his return from the American War, General Dalrymple was appointed His Majesty's Minister Plenitentiary to the King and Republic of Poland. After he was advanced to Prussia, he allowed British relations with the dying Frederick the Great to be steered by his first secretary — with whose policies he did not agree — while he attended to ceremonial matters. He was proudest of serving as First Commissioner to confer the Garter on the Landgrave of Hesse-Cassel (who, during the Revolution, had supplied Hessians who fought the Americans). Dalrymple was soon called home to have his diplomatic career forever drowned by quartermaster troubles which had been mounting in his absence and were to engulf him for another fifteen years.

The accounts of Dyckman's three new clients were at first routinely assigned to the Auditors of Imprest, who had passed those of their predecessors, and, despite apprehensions, did not wish to discredit their earlier reports by admitting a necessity for new departures. Dyckman was emboldened by the ease with which everything was approved to try the "experiment" of charging the Crown for horses which had been shot because they had glanders or other communicative diseases, although during the New York investigation, this expense had been attributed to the owners of the wagons and cited as helping to justify the large sums they received for hire. The Auditors of Imprest docilely checked off £7,000.

However, *The Seventh Report* continued, principally because of

Clinton's protestations, to nod its awful head over the proceedings. He was the more enraged because Cornwallis, whom he considered the instigator of the report, had been appointed governor-general of India while Clinton was allowed no appointment whatsoever. He agitated, even securing partial support from Prime Minister Pitt, to have the investigation reopened so that he could counter Cornwallis's testimony with his own. Dyckman viewed with alarm: "Why revive a business that has given so much trouble? . . . Admitting that it would end in justice to our cause, nothing will be gained that will balance the evil." It was most important for the quartermasters to get, as far as possible, out of the public eye.

Clinton failed to get the *Seventh Report* reopened, but he did publish a defensive book and many pamphlets. Although not centering on the quartermasters' expenses, his writings kept them under discussion. Finally, the Treasury ordered that the Comptrollers' Commission for Auditing the Public Accounts take over, from the more routine Auditors of Imprest, the investigation that was still wrestling inconclusively with the records of Dalrymple's administration.

The new Commission concluded almost at once that what they were examining was not a coat of many colors, from which Dalrymple's garish practices could be detached, but a web, like a knitted fabric, that extended backward at least as far as the arrival of the great expeditionary force under General Howe. In June, 1786, Erskine was informed that the accounts of his administration were to be completely reexamined. As a first step, requisitions totaling £10,240 which had formerly been accepted were, until further evidence was presented, disallowed. This threat to reopen everything brought all the full and deputy quartermasters pelting to London, where they met in a somewhat hysterical conclave with Dyckman and the lawyer, William Adam.

Dyckman's presence being considered essential, the conference was held in his lodgings where he was confined by gout. It was a stormy session. "Well I recollect the want of harmony among you, until Mr. Adam with my assistance stopped the alarming proceedings." Further, more amicable, proceedings were subsequently held.

The Comptrollers' immediate request was for detailed information "with respect to the issuing of fuel, lumber, and all other stores used at the shop and wagon yards." This was aimed at a long-vexed question: had the cost of upkeep and repairs, which was cited by the proprietors as a justification for the high cost of hire, been in fact paid, directly from Crown funds.

Erskine, who always insisted that he had been forced by his military commands to rely on "those who acted with him," wanted to put all the cards on the table: he would rather be out of pocket than appear "dishonorable." This horrified the others. The lawyer William Adam opposed unstinting exposure, but believed that some effort should be made "to satisfy the comptrollers." Dyckman, so he later claimed, was alone in being "fixed and constant in the opinion not to submit to the unjust demand." He argued that there was no middle ground. Were this request agreed to, every account would be "laid open to the examination of the most persecuting tribunal that ever was instituted. . . . My knowledge and experience in the business enabled me positively and successfully to maintain" that the cash accounts, having already been passed by the Auditors of Imprest, "were not subject to the inspection of the comptroller."

One may suspect that Dyckman's "knowledge and experience" had indicated that the comptrollers felt far from comfortable with their demand. Many powerful former officials would be outraged at the summoning up of skeletons from however shallow graves.

Dyckman, furthermore, could offer to sweeten the refusal by satisfying a question he had foreseen which had not been previously settled. When last in New York, he had copied down the records concerning some £100,000 worth of stores which had been shipped from England during Erskine's term. By docilely presenting these figures, he was able to throw a sop to the comptrollers which saved Erskine and the others from "the most perplexing situation imaginable."

During the summer of 1786, Dyckman's much younger brother, William, arrived from the Hudson River valley, sent by the family in part to persuade States to come home. Being able to report in detail on the situation in Westchester, the brother convinced the refugee that the long-looked-forward-to moment had finally come. He would accompany William across the Atlantic when the waters became docile in the spring of 1787. In the meanwhile, many luxuries had to be bought which meant much money to collect.

Although Dyckman's status had risen — he, for instance, represented the quartermasters personally with Sir Henry Clinton — his position remained too inferior for him to set for his "patrons" a price for his services. However, he had learned to use *noblesse oblige* as a fruitful extractor of funds. The secret was to make use of each client's reluctance to be revealed as less generous than the others.

Upon occasion he induced one client to appeal directly to another, an activity towards which Erskine (who would have been most useful) was chary, and Bruen (whose calls could be counterproductive) most eager. The basic technique was for Dyckman to communicate to client B that client A had given him so and so much which B would surely wish to match. Then on to C. It was advantageous to raise, citing some act along the way of actual or presumed further generosity, the ante so that by the time the circle got back to A, he would have further to sweeten the pot. Dyckman did not feel impelled to communicate more than was to his advantage: He allowed himself to receive twice over his expenses in London, which he calculated at £250 a year.

More direct appeals to a single patron could also be effective. Although Bruen was the most generous, Erskine was the rock: he arranged to give his protégé an annuity which he increased from £60 to £100 a year. (There was no way of knowing that what was intended to protect the extravagant man for the rest of his life would carry him to the very brink of disaster.) Dalrymple, whom States truly pitied, was always running frightened, and thus open to request, but he was often out of funds. The good-natured Robertson needed only to be asked. Cathcart was the tough nut to crack. Finally driven to breach the system, Dyckman sicced an attorney on the Noble Lord. The Noble Lord objected that he found it "disagreeable . . . to enter into a pecuniary negotiation with a gentleman I am a stranger to." Had he known Dyckman needed money he would have given him some. However, he sent nothing but "best wishes." Eventually, he promised £200.

Dyckman placed £2,000 of what he collected in the funds. The earnings from this capital (which he swore never to touch) plus the annuity from Erskine, would, so he wrote to Samson, enable him, "according to my ideas of happiness and the prices of the conveniences of life in America" to foresee a happy futurity without being troubled with "gloomy apprehensions." The £200 Cathcart had agreed to give him would pay his passage home and enable him to set up on his farm. That left quantities of money to spend, and he spent them. Before he got back to America he alienated thousands of pounds.

As Dyckman prepared to sail in the summer of 1787 he paid for redecorating much of Mrs. Tait's house. He gave his brother William securities worth £500. The easily portable objects he bought included a forty-one-piece tea set in white and gold china, quantities of glassware, more and more dining room silver, prints to be elegantly framed, by the score. Probably because the veneers essential to eighteenth-century cabinetmaking might peel off during an ocean voyage, he bought no furniture. Although his writings do not reveal him as a reader, he had acquired since his return to London an extensive library. One list — the expert accountant reveled in keeping lists — showed thirty quarto and sixty octavo volumes on "divinity and ecclesiastical history." The mix on "poetry, poetical translation and dramatic works" was fifteen large and one hundred eighty small. Other categories were history, natural history, chronology, biography, topography, antiquities, and miscellaneous. He considered that he had a complete "gentleman's library except for military books and French authors." So that the volumes would make an impressive display when shelved, he had them identically and expensively bound.

Although Dyckman had also reserved passage for himself, during May, 1787, William went off alone. Even if not so continuously that he lacked the time for expensive jaunts to France and Holland, States was held by a new crisis, this time between the quartermasters themselves.

The issue, which had long been festering, concerned what had happened when Dalrymple had arrived in New York to take over as quartermaster general. He brought so little money — or so Bruen claimed — that Bruen had to lend him £500 to buy his share as proprietor. His patron, Clinton, being in South Carolina besieging Charleston, Dalrymple then sailed south, where he arranged with the wagon master, McNair, that all the proprietors' profits be paid personally to him. Bruen charged that Dalrymple had sent the £36,000 directly to his London bankers without giving Bruen and Robertson each his rightful third. Dalrymple replied that they had been paid.

During March of 1787, Dyckman undertook undercover work for Bruen. In seeming to be pursuing his routine duties, he questioned McNair, whose answers neither he nor Bruen believed. Alas, Dyckman could not attempt to examine Dalrymple's bank account "lest it should cause jealousy." Bruen and Robertson should search their own accounts to make sure neither had received a payment of £12,000. Bruen's reply was a bellow of denial. Robertson was so "distressed" he could not do anything for a while and then found his accounts fuzzy. "To the best of my knowledge" he had not been paid, but he was not sure. Everything remained up in the air, but States could point out to Bruen that his abandoning his trip home was "another instance that nothing shall interfere with my duty to you."

Dyckman turned down an offer — it would have kept him in England — to establish him in the wine business, and asked Bruen's permission finally to depart. Bruen replied with such a diatribe of hurt feelings that States agreed to stay until the following spring. In reporting this to Samson, he asked his brother to placate his mother (no mention of Caty)* by informing her that his staying on was motivated by gratitude rather than any hope of further gain.

Even to his brother, States was extremely discreet about the business he was engaged in. He did not mention that the quartermasters were facing the long-dreaded worst possible threat. Since the basic issue had always been whether they had drained off greater profits than the unwritten laws of prerogative allowed, nothing could be really decided, however much the surface was combed and recombed, without determining how great the profit had actually been. Various estimates had been made, but always Dyckman and his colleagues had been able to cast doubt on the figures. From the very first, the need had been to seek access to the proprietors' "private" books, and this the

---

* Caty's husband, with his usual brisk assumption of family right, had drawn on States for an additional £450 so that he could buy a lot on which to build his store. States would, of course, agree that any security was unnecessary because of his brother-in-law's obvious rectitude.

Comptrollers finally decided to do. They found, they thought, a way to go about it that would not elicit from other uneasy public officials a cry of "foul." They would induce Dalrymple to *volunteer* the information.

The attack was double. On July 30, 1787, the Attorney and Solicitor General informed Dalrymple that it would be to his advantage to join with them in a recommendation "to His Majesty to grant his sign manual for passing this account according to such rate of hire as they shall think reasonable upon inquiry and in consideration of the facts in the *Seventh Report*." Although Dalrymple's tormentors agreed to calculate in what they considered a profit suitable for a public official who had carried out his duties efficiently, this would force returning a very large sum of money. Dalrymple's obvious riposte was to present, if it could be done in any way to his advantage, papers from his private books.

The intention was made more specific by another directive: the Comptrollers would not accept Dalrymple's official accounts without demonstration from the other set of books that the horses and wagons had actually been bought and had remained in service.

Dalrymple was not, of course, left to make his decision alone. The other quartermasters and the lawyers gathered around him. Dyckman urged a bold insistence that the Comptrollers had no authority whatsoever to demand private books. Otherwise, they might "discover the profit, a discovery we are advised by no means to gratify them with."

The lawyers, however, decided to take no stand on principle. Dalrymple's reply merely stated that the books were not in his possession nor could he achieve access to them. Fortunately, so the paper continued, the investigators already had all the evidence they needed: the expenditures had been ordered by the commander in chief; and the evidence of two officials appointed by the commander in chief, who were not proprietors, supported "the veracity of the signatures of the drivers."

The Comptrollers answered that they would not accept Dalrymple's statement that he did not have access to the private books. Dalrymple then wavered, wondering whether he could not extract some evidence that would prove to his advantage. The other quartermasters reacted with horror: Dalrymple's accounts could not be separated from those of the whole Department.

Preparing to fall back, lest it prove necessary, on the uncompromising stand which Dyckman had recommended, the lawyers concluded that "no power" — not even, Dyckman wrote, "God" — could force disclosure. They contended that the quartermasters' private books had no relevance to their public trust. This was because every quartermaster had been for legal purposes two people: as a proprietor, he had not rented to himself but to a quartermaster.

By chance or by foresight, the books had been left at New York in the possession of the Department's agents, Winthrop & Kemble. New York was now deliciously beyond the power of British law, yet the Comptrollers might try to bamboozle the papers from the agents. And Dalrymple might ask to be sent specific records, thus not only compromising his associates but breaking the united front. Again, the spotlight of the negotiation was moving across the ocean to the delight of Dyckman, who was eager to get home without damaging his position with his clients.

Dyckman pointed out that Winthrop & Kemble were completely uninformed concerning the developments in London. They could not know the significance of a requisition from some high official of the Crown or from Dalrymple, who had been one of their employers and would seem to have a right to receive his papers if he wanted them. Surely, it would be prudent to have Dyckman at the agents' side, advising. Bruen, forever suspicious of his fellow quartermasters, urged that Dyckman, while he was with the agents, look into the division of the spoils. This required (or supplied an excuse for) his carrying with him across the ocean the "trunkful" of incriminating papers that were to play so important a role in the remainder of his career and in the writing of this volume.

Dyckman further sped his departure by informing the quartermasters that he had received warnings from his friends in the Comptroller's office "that they have it in mind to examine me verbally. My absence . . . may be a prudent measure."

The call for a rapid departure dictated a winter voyage that would be for him deeply unfortunate. He was harassed with gout which struck particularly in cold weather. He decided to serve "both health and curiosity" by taking a southern route: via Portugal, Madeira and Jamaica to Charleston, where he would arrive when spring was enlivening the countryside. This itinerary had a built-in danger: pirates. So that, as a friend cheerfully put it, he would be able to "cut a figure among the Algerians if you are carried there," he bought insurance that would keep him from being treated and sold as a slave.

After an English stay that had lasted, with one considerable interruption, for eleven years, the former Loyalist set out during December, 1788, for the new nation which he had opposed and which had won freedom while he was away serving the enemy.

◯

CHAPTER TEN

The Refugee Dares

DYCKMAN had made sure that the *Polly* was "a fast sailer." And, indeed, she carried him to Lisbon without disastrous intervention by pirates. However, he was assailed by his own body. Gout struck almost as soon as the ship left England. As the vessel lay "directly opposite the city, within one hundred yards of the shore" Dyckman was "lashed to my berth by both feet." He could not walk or stand. How he wished he had never left London! "The contrast between the happy hours I had passed both in George Street and Gloucestershire [where Mrs. Tait's relations lived] and the heavy ones" he was "compelled to sigh away, was so great and so painful that I cannot bear even the recollections."

After nine days, States was able to get ashore. He took lodgings "on top of the highest hill in Lisbon. . . . This house is kept by a Mrs. Dorr, an Irish lady, and is extremely clean and comfortable." From one window, he looked over the river Tagus to where the ancient castle at Alfama, "celebrated in verse and history," crowned a perpendicular cliff. Another window "commands the entrance to the river, and the castles which defend it, together with a vast extent of the Atlantic. A third window gives me a view of the city, which at a little distance has a pleasing appearance. The churches and houses are all built of white stone or rather marble, and from the unevenness of the ground seem to

[109]

be pitched upon one another in the greatest confusion. The city has been almost entirely rebuilt since the last quake. In some places, the ruins of that dreadful shock are still to be seen, and the appearance is truly awful. . . .

"The pureness of the air and the amazing appetite it gave me soon recovered me the use of my feet and with them my spirits. I no longer wished myself back in England. . . . I never felt myself in better health. . . . As I had the precaution to bring a few letters with me, I have not a day without an engagement."

When he went on to Madeira, he carried letters from his new friends in Lisbon. They in turn gave him letters to use at his next destination: "The pleasure of Mr. Dyckman's company will be the best apology for this intrusion."

The man who had spent so much time and money in London on tasteful purchases, did not seek out connoisseurs or collectors. He preferred "hearty" companions, who would take him on "jaunts." In his extensive travel journal the son of an orchardist was more concerned with exotic trees than with elegant furnishings.

The long leg of his journey was the three-and-a-half-months' crossing to the island of Jamaica. His own gout did not return, but it was hardly cheering to have one of his few fellow passengers die of gout, and watch the weighted body vanish under the ocean.

Here is his description of a climb in Jamaica. "The first ascent seemed frightful. But we had no sooner got beyond this hill but we entered the most rural and beautiful wood I ever saw. The air was perfumed with fragrance of the flowing shrubs and blossoms of limes, oranges, etc., and the nightingales, or rather the American mocking birds, here enjoyed a perpetual spring and seemed to express their thanks in notes more sweet and musical than Billington or Mara. The road was diversified by sometimes ascending a lofty hill (but always shaded with cotton trees) and sometimes winding down the valleys, ever green. Streams of water were only wanting in those enchanting vales to make them answer to the description of Milton's *Paradise*. The road was in general a strip of red earth running between borders of green. As the shade of the lofty trees permitted the dew to lie till near twelve it was soft and cool to the horses' feet as well as refreshing to the traveler's eye. There are very few plantations in these mountains, but many *pens* where stocks are raised in such abundance that the island can now depend upon itself and hardly needs the assistance of other countries. In a short time the whole island will be taken in hand and rendered useful, much to the general benefit."

Following winds sped his voyage from Jamaica to Norfolk, Virginia. Traveling from there overland, he reached the banks of the Hudson on January 11, 1789.

Eager as he was to greet his relations after so long a separation — his mother had grown pitifully older during the almost twelve intervening years — States was also eager to examine the farm which Samson had bought at his request to be his future home. He was glad to confirm that the land was not embedded in the wild scenery which dominated so much of the Hudson River valley. What became during the nineteenth century the inspiration of the most famous school of American landscape painters was repulsive to accepted eighteenth-century taste. Concerning a house perched over the river on one of the cliffs, a diarist, James Thacher, wrote during the Revolution that it might appeal to someone "guided altogether by a taste for romantic singularity and novelty." It was "surrounded on two sides by hideous mountains and dreary forests, not a house in view but one within a mile."

Dyckman, making while in Jamaica the connoisseur's distinction between the "beautiful" and "the grand or sublime," ruled strongly for the first. He felt uneasy in vistas "where the eye in vain searches for green fields and pleasant streams." How fortunate that his farm was far from the wild and strange. Indeed, the mildness of the landscape had dictated that a road which passed through his property was among the most frequented in rural America.

A few miles upriver, passage of traffic across the Hudson was barred by the flanking mountains. A few miles downriver, the Hudson opened out into a small inland ocean. Although in the twentieth century this shallow expanse is crossed by the tremendous Tappan Zee Bridge, in the eighteenth century the wide bay was difficult and sometimes, because of freakish winds, dangerous to cross.

When States walked through his fields past his salt marsh down to the riverbank, the drop was gradual. The west shore was close, and over his right shoulder the crossing was narrowed by a promontory: Verplanck's Point. Across the river, there was also a promontory: Stony Point. Between these, he saw a constant movement of ferryboats, often carrying loaded teams. This was King's Ferry, a river crossing of much more continental import than the Harlem River span States's father had built years before to help link Manhattan to the mainland.

The Hudson was the major river barrier in the then United States. Rising from the northern wilderness and disgorging into the Atlantic Ocean, it cut the United States in half. During the recent war, the revolutionaries had built forts on both Stony and Verplanck's points. These were captured by the British in 1779, a stroke which George Washington considered "certainly one of the wisest measures" ever pursued by the enemy. Alexander Hamilton explained that in losing King's Ferry the Americans had lost "our best communication between the eastern and southern states."

A secret, midnight expedition commanded by General Anthony Wayne recaptured Stony Point, but an effort to extend the triumph to Verplanck's Point failed. Even Stony Point had to be surrendered almost instantly as the British navy came up the river. However, Wayne's success in beating up the garrison made the British conclude that they could not safely occupy posts so deep in disputed territory. During the fall of 1779, they permanently abandoned their effort to control King's Ferry. When Dyckman arrived, the fort on Verplanck's Point had been altered into a dwelling house where Samson lived complainingly and uncomfortably: the roof leaked.

Of two roads connecting King's Ferry with the Albany Post Road and thus much of settled America, one ran through States's farm. Had his father lived, the parent would undoubtedly have volubly argued that here was the perfect spot for such a voluminously profitable tavern as would, had it come his way, have made his fortune. States had made his own fortune, and had no intention of becoming an innkeeper. However, the recent arrival from London undoubtedly enjoyed the traffic that, without disturbing the inner peace of his farmland, moved by his door. And he could not regret that thousands would admire the improvements he intended to make in the existing farmhouse.

With glances to the ferry below and back across the ocean, he determined to name his new property King's Grange.

Dyckman's first essential task was to get in touch with the firm of Winthrop & Kemble. As he had expected, the Commissioners had applied to them for the quartermasters' private books. Winthrop expressed himself as "truly astonished at . . . their impertinent request." Dyckman considered the refusal Winthrop had already sent the Commissioners "a very proper one." The agent assured Dyckman that he would never supply the British government with any papers. But what, Dyckman asked, if Dalrymple requested certain documents? Winthrop would never satisfy Dalrymple without the approval of all the proprietors.

Dyckman had promised Bruen that he would not correspond directly with Dalrymple. He sent the news to the lawyer, William Hamilton, asking to be kept informed. There is no indication that he busied himself with carrying out his mission of proving that Bruen had been cheated.

Despite all the assurances he had been given, Dyckman was far from certain that he would find it safe or agreeable to stay permanently in America. Looking anxiously around him, he was delighted to identify as the resident menaces not bloodthirsty anti-Loyalists but little bugs destroying the wheat and Indian corn. The Constitution had been ratified: Washington was President. Diagnosing "a change in the disposition of the people, an alteration much for the better," he wrote that he was surrounded with "everything I could wish except for the poverty of the farmers."

The British traveler William Strickland documents that poverty. Of States's neighborhood, he wrote: The houses "are in general way much out of repair, and there is an appearance of want of substance in the owners which disables them from improving their houses and cultivating their lands. They seem in general to possess little more than mere necessities. Not a gentleman's seat is met with between Dobbs Ferry and Peekskill."

States quickly decided that he wished to let "my days terminate here." He was not bothered, as were his neighbors, by any lack of money. However, as he settled down on his farm, he made no efforts to create "a gentleman's seat." He merely acquired some additional land, and added to the old farmhouse "a small, convenient" addition. By December, he was able to attach "paper borders" to the newly painted walls.

What he created during the next four and a half years was thus described by Strickland in 1794: a farm of 240 acres, "improved as far as possible according to the ideas of the country." It was "in a high state of cultivation . . . and extremely well planted with the best kind of fruit trees, now in high condition and full bearing, with a good house upon it."

The fermentable liquor from States's cider mill seems to have been mostly for home consumption, but his sawmills served the neighborhood: the sawyer paid him 50 percent of the profits. John Chatterton, who plowed the fields, also supplied the seed. Hay was stored in "the barracks": four vertical poles from which hung a roof that could be raised or lowered to accommodate the stack. States usually employed two farmhands, others being hired by the day when needed. He owned slaves, at least periodically: a doctor's bill included inoculating five negroes and "delivering Jude's baby." The bachelor household was presided over by Sarah Wilkinson (known as Sill), who remained a beloved member of the Dyckman family.

Having moved from the money economy of London to the American countryside, Dyckman often paid his bills in goods: most frequently bushels of wheat and rye, sometimes bars of iron that could be worked into useful objects by a blacksmith. He bought yards of cloth wholesale and cut pieces to sizes that met specific debts. His bills reveal no purchases from New York cabinetmakers. Since he had brought no furniture with him from England, he must have arranged his imported silver and pewter and china and glass in American country settings. No finely crafted bookshelves housed his large holding of elaborately and identically bound books. A "German voice flute" was one of the few objects of taste he bought. Typical purchases: buckskin gloves, a sportsman's knife, gunpowder, fishing tackle. However, it can be doubted that States was greatly given to outdoor exercise. He had never been an athletic man and had returned from London a chronic, if intermittent, invalid.

Many citizens of the twentieth century can enjoy the luxury of regarding gout as a semi-comic ailment attacking the big toes of old gentlemen who drink too much port. In Dyckman's eighteenth century, gout was a devastating scourge. Among innumerable others, it killed the era's greatest statesman, William Pitt. Why the ailment has shrunk to minor proportions is one of the mysteries of epidemiology. Modern science is ignorant of the fundamental causes of the condition and possesses only palliatives to fight it.

Gout is a metabolic disorder caused by the release into the body of uric acid normally discharged with urine. The excess acid deposits crystals in the joints, crippling with pain. (It is not known why the agony usually appears first in the big toe.) The continuing metabolic disproportion damages the functioning of vital organs to an extent that can be fatal.

During the first years of States's return to America, his gout was not life-endangering. However, there was no foreseeing when it would cripple an arm or a leg or how long an attack would last. When it was present, the pain was excruciating. Gout is one of the most painful ailments known to man.

As he had sailed away from England, Dyckman had left behind orders that his London agents should violate the rules under which he had for so long operated. If any of his clients did not meet their written promises, they were to be taken, like unexalted delinquents, to court. How he would enjoy sponsoring a suit against Lord Cathcart! He could "hardly bring [himself] to come to extremities with General Dalrymple," yet, if Dalrymple delayed payment for more than six months, "delicacy . . . must give way to justice." As his bankers informed him, the money was collected without any unseemly explosions.

The man who, despite the passage of years and his haven at Mrs. Tait's, had been in London always an alien, was gathered up into a tight family circle. Dyckman's brothers, Samson, Benjamin and William, and his widowed sister, Mrs. Vredenburgh, all lived in the neighborhood; there were nephews and nieces and cousins; his mother, old and infirm, had her own house but periodically stayed with her children. The welfare of States's close relatives was considered the responsibility of all. "On my return to this country," States was later to complain, "I found numerous sets of relations all ruined and beggared by the war. It was natural for me to assist them, but probably imprudent to the extent that I did. As, however, I felt not immediately the effects of it, it did not distress me." What distressed him almost beyond bearing were the tribulations of his sister Caty.

❧

CHAPTER ELEVEN

Drug Addiction

DYCKMAN could not have been long home before he saw Caty in her married condition. She was overjoyed to welcome him, but sickly and dispirited. Her husband proved as self-righteous and energetic as his letters had foretold. But States could diagnose a cringing behind his aggressiveness. Far from being sympathetic with Caty's drooping weakness, Hale was enraged by it.

The brother-in-law called himself Major Hale, but his claim to that considerable rank in the Continental Army cannot be substantiated in the standard records. The Dyckman family, States was to assert, had "first lifted him up from nothing and afterwards supported him." Funds procured from States had, indeed, bought the partnership in Robertson and Hale, "dealers in West Indian and European goods," and also the conspicuous lot in Albany, "opposite the Dutch church," on which the store had been built. Still owing much of the money and hoping to borrow more, Hale had strong reasons to ingratiate himself to his brother-in-law. True, the contrast between the glowing looks Caty gave her dear States and "the terrible countenance" which she often turned on him was hardly agreeable. However, Hale nourished the hope that States would use his influence with Caty to make her behave towards her husband as what he considered a dutiful wife.

Caty hoped that her brother's return would in some miraculous way make her life bearable. If only the intervention of her beloved States would smooth her domestic difficulties, enabling her to please her husband and be an exemplary wife and mother!

States was distressed that his sister was so unhappy. He wished to help heal the bleeding wounds in her marriage. Yet he enjoyed having her come to King's Grange for long visits. The complaining and contentious Hale was not a man whom the skilled conciliator ever could have liked, and there was every reason to resent the blusterer's behavior to the sister whom States had cherished ever since she was an infant.

Hale, who liked to talk and write about himself and was convinced that all "persons of common sense, feeling, and liberality" would approve "every transaction" of his life, was only too eager to expose his attitudes and behavior towards Caty. He had, he admitted, been unpleasantly upset at the start of the marriage, but he had explained to Caty his reasons (they seem to have been financial before States came to the rescue) which he insisted were beyond censure. He had soon become "as composed in mind as nine-tenths of mankind." However, Caty had allowed her own state of mind, "for no apparent reason," to become such as made "everyone miserable around you, and myself, as your nearest connection, most completely so."

Difficulties in his business, he admitted, still made him sometimes irritable, but the fact that he was preserving his wife and children from "want" placed on the wife an inescapable duty. "Have I not reason to expect and demand of you," he asked in a letter to Caty which he was glad to show around, "as the partner of my life and fortunes, that whenever you see me disturbed at disappointments in business and any other cause be it what it may, that you endeavor to soothe my peace of mind and join me in correcting, as far as lies in your power, any causes I may have for uneasiness." As it was, her "sullen gloomy countenance" took his mind off his business and deprived his household of peace.

Furthermore, as she lay sick in bed, she neglected domestic economy, adding to costs.

These charges, along with endless others — Caty was jealous of a former flame concerning whom Hale had in "candor" dilated to her; she accused Hale's sister of scheming against her — were unrolled in endless letters aimed, so Hale explained, at establishing a foundation for future happiness by convincing Caty that, although he himself had his minor weaknesses (which he regretted), in all serious ways she was altogether in the wrong. The screeds never state or imply love, and promise "affection" only in return for reformation and good behavior. No consideration is given to the possibility that Caty might have nerves or emotions of her own. That she failed in her duty to sit by his fireside with "a cheerful countenance . . . mild and serene, indicating peace within and good will all around," was due to stubborn wickedness.

As neurotic as her husband, habituated by States to the greatest admiration and the tenderest support, Caty had become, while States was still in London, more and more unhappy. Enter Dr. Samuel Stringer. Stringer had much more to account for than his disastrous effect on Caty's life and by extension the life of States Dyckman. Had it not been for his ministrations, Canada might today be part of the United States.

When the Revolutionary War had broken out, the British had failed to prepare Canada for defense. Two patriot armies — one led by Benedict Arnold — were sent to capture the province. They were repelled not by any military force, but by the results of a controversy within the Medical Department of the Continental Army. The Department was presumably under the direction of the most brilliant doctor in America, John Morgan, a European-trained experimenter who had in Philadelphia founded the continent's first medical school. He was opposed as a big-city snob with fancy ideas by the largely self-trained rural practitioners who had marched to the war with local regiments. Placing himself at the head of this opposition, Stringer had managed to wrest away from Morgan command of the Medical Department in Canada. Some historians, including this writer in his *Doctors on Horseback*, have blamed on Stringer's incompetence the epidemics that reduced the patriots to a pitiful remnant fleeing back across the border. After that, British forces having come in, it was too late.

Stringer's reputation as a physician had remained high in his native Albany. Caty sought from him the cure for "a painful indisposition." He recommended to her, as the "readiest method to halt pain," laudanum drops (a tincture of opium). She was to insist that Stringer had supplied the drops "as a medicine without her ever knowing at first what the consequence was." In upshot, "the ease she desired from them naturally made her want to continue on the use of them." There was then no restriction on the sale. She became addicted.

For several years, during which Caty kept much to her room as an invalid, no one (in Hale's words) "knew the pernicious effect of the drops, or indeed, what was the medicine which you so frequently sent for." The mystery had not been elucidated when States returned from England.

Not so long thereafter, one of Caty's relations discovered the truth. She told States, who volunteered that the next time Caty visited him he would keep her at King's Grange until she was "weaned" from the drops. Hale's sister, who was also told, agreed that the facts should be withheld from her brother; he was so easily upset and already so outdone with his wife. States did his best but Caty proved immune to rapid weaning. Thus was set the scene for a drama which Hale cited over and over as a grievance against Caty.

Hale was traveling to Albany on one of the sloops that carried passengers and produce up and down the Hudson. The vessel docked at King's Ferry where Caty and States were waiting.

Caty announced that she was determined to return to her family, although her brother wished her to stay over. "Shortly thereafter" Hale went ashore with States. Returning, he told her with great agitation that she was to get off and stay with her brother. When she asked why, he replied that he now knew she was taking laudanum and had agreed that her brother was to cure her. She then, so Hale reiterated, "assumed that strange appearance and behavior . . . which vexed and mortified me beyond expression and must have filled all the passengers with surprise and disgust. . . . You instantly flew into a passion and said you would then stay away entirely. I answered you coolly you must act your pleasure. You replied you would not stay at King's Ferry but go somewhere else. I answered you could go where you pleased. . . . Reflect now for one moment what were the countenance and manner you put on toward me! I candidly acknowledge that I never longed with more anxiety . . . than I then did for your disembarking, that I might lose sight of a countenance so completely disagreeable to me." It was only because of "the misery and distress of mind I cannot help feeling upon all these occasions" that he ever treated his wife "with neglect and unkindness."

Caty did stay at King's Grange and her brother continued to try. Neither he nor anybody else realized the seriousness of the problem. The cure, it was believed, required no more than persuading the delinquent to use self-control. When States caught Caty behaving in the manner she admitted was so deleterious, he scolded and appealed to her better nature. Since she was not confined to the house and no laws restricted the sale of laudanum, she kept herself adequately supplied.

For a while, Caty periodically returned home. She wrote States from Albany, "I have to answer your letter . . . but I was so affected with reading your letter that I could not. I can assure you that I was not displeased with you for writing as you did, though I could have wished that you had saved yourself the trouble and me the pain. . . . The impropriety of my past conduct I see as plain as you or any person can paint to me, and the recollection of it is almost too much for my poor intellects to bear with calmness, and I must request of you that you will say nothing to me on the subject of what is past for six months and allow me that time to wean myself from the drops which I have been seven years* accustomed to take. You may suppose what my feelings must be when I do not take them, and what pain I would not under go rather than persevere in taking them, contrary to my own inclination and against the wishes of my friends. I will exert myself all I can for my own sake and more for your and my poor husband's sake, and what would I not do for my dear children's sake!

"After I had read your letter I burnt it as I thought you did not wish any other person to see it except myself, but Mr. Hale came in the room at the time and seeing me very much distressed and knowing at what, requested to see the letter. I told him I had burnt it and told him as well as I could the subject and what it contained, but he did not appear to be satisfied and I wish you would acquaint him with the contents for my sake.

"I shall expect you up next week. Give my love to all the family, and permit me to tell you I love you more than I can express, and that I will do all I can to merit your esteem."

Caty was in so pitiful a condition that her presence could only give pain. Her husband came to feel that his sensitive nerves — did he not owe to his family the tranquility necessary to carry on his business? — could not bear having her in the house. He exiled his wife to King's Ferry, even allowing her little son William to go along. States felt that in taking care of his sister he was

---

*This figure is clearly an exaggeration since it would have carried Caty back to before she was in Albany with Hale and Dr. Stringer.

"serving" his brother-in-law. However, Hale was not grateful. Was not States coming between him and his wife?

Fearing to express anger to the man who held a mortgage on his store, Hale turned all his fury on Caty, firing off letters each of which "occasioned a fit that lasted for several days." Still regarding herself as a loyal wife, she did not show her brother the letters. Finally, States wrote Hale suggesting that he communicate with the sufferer in a less upsetting style. Hale responded by sending States a copy of one of his letters: a denunciation of a hundred past derelictions running to thousands of words.

States commented, "After reading this, you may well suppose I had little hopes of my sister's happiness. Indeed, I was not surprised that she had recourse to laudanum to lose her sorrow in stupefaction." Hale's "cruelty had nearly damaged her reason." Caty remained in a state of pulverized confusion and misery.

So matters drifted along in unmitigated unhappiness and anger until in January, 1791, Elizabeth Dyckman Blake, the relation who had first recognized the situation, decided to take determined steps. Securing the agreement of Caty, who nonetheless moaned that "it would be fatal to her," she made "a trial of the consequences" of separating the addict altogether from the drug. "The anguish," she wrote Hale, "was indeed alarming. For three days she was continually delirious and wracked with excruciating pain that a stone could not look at her without pity." Finally, panic-stricken, the sister sent for some drops although "I almost despaired at her taking them or anything else." She was able to take them, and the agony abated.

Then, at long last, a real effort was made to get sophisticated medical advice. The first doctor consulted said, "If she was ever to be weaned from them it must be the work of time and done by small graduations." Mrs. Blake "procured some drops from him, and also some medicine to dilute it." A second physician enforced a greater reduction of the drug, at which Caty was "taken so ill" that a third was called in. He increased the allowance "by a few drops."

Hale's reaction to this news was to announce bravely: "I find myself master of more firmness than I could have supposed possible had I not been put to the painful trial."

Laudanum now disappears as a major concern in the continuing correspondence, but Caty's condition had clearly not been stabilized on any level that permitted happiness. Her husband continued to throw fuel on her sense of guilt. She nurtured a passionate desire to be forgiven and allowed to come home.

In 1792, Caty wrote her husband: "My brother will convince you that I am unable at present to answer your letter fully as I wished or as you may desire. Indeed, there are some passages in it which I do not understand — at the time you say you expected a letter from me. I had no reason to think that you expected or wished me to write to you, and I as much expected from time to time to hear from or to see you till I knew not what to think — and what any person or persons could tell you to prejudice you against me I cannot think. My mother has been ill since last fall and most part of the winter her life has been despaired of, and I watched her day and night and never left her till a few days before my brother's [Samson's] death I went to see him and take leave of him — a melancholy and dreary winter to me in every particular. But as it is impossible for me to write any ways satisfactory to myself or you, I beg that you will come to me before you return to Albany. This I request in the most earnest manner, and be assured that you will not find me backward to confess whatever has been amiss in my conduct — I beg you will let no consideration prevent your having an interview with me. If you do not, you will never see me I am fully convinced, and to leave this world in the situation I am with you at present is a reflection too melancholy for my spirits to support with calmness. If you think proper to come, which I trust you will, I could wish you could be here before the company arrives which my brother expects from New York. And may heaven assist me in my endeavors to convince you that I would do anything to contribute to your peace or contentment as well as to my dear States, whose love to me I am sure in all my sickness and pains never could be excelled by any friend or brother — God I trust will reward him for it. I will conclude with my wishes to see you as soon as you may think proper and your business will permit you to come. . . .

"If I have not wrote agreeable to your wishes, attribute it to my expecting to see you and endeavoring to satisfy you in every particular, and assure yourself there is nothing in this world I so anxiously wish for — you certainly know if you consider that I have not fortitude nor strength of mind to carry on a correspondence of this nature with you — your letters distress me so that I have not fortitude scarcely to read them, how then can I sit down and answer them as you wish?"

Hale, so States insisted, never ceased torturing his wife. He would encourage her hopes that he would take her back, and then, launching terrific charges, dash her hopes. After he managed to get rid of the impeding mortgage — States claimed he had evaded payment by a trick — he emerged as a full-fledged enemy of the Dyckman family. To defend himself in Albany against imputations that he had deserted his wife, Hale, assisted by his sister, blamed everything on States: the marriage had been a perfect success and would have continued so had not the brother intervened. Because of States, his wife had become incapable of carrying out her domestic duties. She was a helpless invalid who had to be kept in seclusion. Thus, the ever-loving husband was sentenced by his interfering brother-in-law to eternal loneliness.

Hale saw no contradiction in charging that the woman he defined as a helpless invalid was committing adultery with whatever man he heard had been in her company — a friend of States's named Hill; Green, a schoolmaster who lodged temporarily at the King's Grange; Dr. Eustice, who gave her treatments. In 1794, Hale employed one of New York's leading lawyers, the Federalist leader Josiah Ogden Hoffman, to threaten divorce. The injured husband, Hoffman wrote, possessed plenty of evidence. Hale, who could never keep his mouth closed, revealed that his star witness was a maid whom he had once sent down from Albany to help take care of his wife. Pointing out that he had quickly called the maid back to him, States charged that the maid was Hale's mistress. She was a whore, who had been seen going into a bagnio in New York, and with whom Hale had misbehaved on a New York–to–Albany sloop.

The Dyckmans went before justices of the peace to sign affidavits testifying to Caty's purity. Hoffman sent reiterated legal threats, perpetually disturbing Caty and States, without undertaking any legal action from which they could defend themselves. Although Hale did not dare approach States's house, when Caty was visiting one of her other relatives, he would suddenly appear, loud with upbraidings and charges.

Despite her occasional visits elsewhere, Caty made her home with States. Hour after hour, day after day, year after year, the perpetual tragedy of his ailing, miserable, battered, and beloved sister was played over and over again in the "convenient" farmhouse States had envisioned, when he escaped from London, as a retreat from the rigors of the world. He came to hate Hale with a passion that burst easily into hysteria, but his malign brother-in-law was forever present as an invisible, diabolic companion of the sister he loved. Heroically, he kept her at his hearth as he held her in his heart, but the perpetual strain contributed to a dramatic change in States Dyckman's character.

CHAPTER TWELVE

༄

Marriage to a Girl

T HE voluminous Dyckman Papers contain until September,
1794, no letter he wrote to anyone — client, relation,
friend, or possible enemy — which contains the slightest cutting
edge. Always he is charming and conciliatory. When, shortly
before States left England, Samson had embarrassed him by fail-
ing to pay a debt, he apologized at having called at the wrong
time on his brother to whose comfort he would be happy to ad-
minister at any time. Even Caty's problems with her husband
had not in their early stages elicited any written vituperation
from States.

The first angry letter is to his orphaned niece, Samson's
daughter Catalina, whom States disinherited for projecting a
marriage of which he did not approve.

When his widowed sister displeased him, States showed her
his will "to convince her to what extent her ingratitude had
gone." He accused his brother William of having "very much the
appearance of that of a rogue. . . . I no longer intend to be a
lackey running after you. If the deed is not delivered here in
three days may my soul never enter heaven if I do not publish
your infamous conduct in the newspapers."

This change in Dyckman's temper is the more remarkable
because it coincided with a revolution in his life which should
have brought reassurance and peace.

On a neighboring farm there lived a family named Corne (spelt phonetically in the neighborhood *Corney*). The permanent residents were a grandfather in his seventies, and a granddaughter in her teens.

States could hardly ever have seen a fiercer countenance than Peter Corne's. From beneath inflamed eyelids, ice-blue eyes, although watery with age, glowed hostilely. His prominent nose, almost knife-narrow at the bridge, hooked over strong nostrils. Because his teeth were gone his cheeks were shriveled. His sunken mouth, a downward curve with the extremities pulled inward, preserved an expression of anger. A boulderlike chin bottomed his face.

The granddaughter's appearance was an utter contrast. Elizabeth Corne Kennedy, known as Betsey, had dark red hair which she allowed to fall girlishly, naturally, unfashionably along her back. Curling locks came forward to frame her young face. She had inherited her grandfather's blue eyes, but they were deeper in color, ultramarine and trusting. Her delicate nose was long and straight, continuing the line of her forehead. Although not richly formed, her mouth was both gentle and firm. As her body came into full flower, the heaviness of her breasts accentuated a narrow waist. The smiles she turned on States were warm, shy, and a little arch.

Corne fitted his fierce countenance. The violence of his character is exemplified in a letter he later wrote Dyckman regarding Britain's conciliatory attitude towards Bonaparte: "The genius of Great Britain looks black in the face — her head seems to be in a noose and may be strangled; her glory and pride prostrate on the ground and trampled on by the unhallowed hooves of *sans-culottism*."

Born in 1722 at the English seaport of Hull, Corne came to New York as "a master mariner," and entered into a partnership with important merchants, Anthony and Isaac Van Dam. But he could not bear to sit in the countinghouse. Commanding com-

pany ships to the African coast, he bargained at the pens enclosing captured blacks to secure prime human merchandise which
he carried in the hold of his vessel to the West Indies where the
high mortality on the sugar plantations insured a perpetual mar-
ket. During King George's War (the American offshoot of the
War of the Austrian Succession) Corne was part owner of several
privateers and himself commanded, with a commission from the
Colony of New York, the brigantine *Nebuchadnezzar*, using his
eight guns in hunting French and Dutch merchantmen.

In 1751, Corne had married Elizabeth's grandmother, Elizabeth Henderson, who was a double heiress. Her maternal grandfather, Derrick Benson, was a rich New Jersey landowner.
James Henderson, her father, once a doctor at the hospital at
Greenwich, England, became in New York City a very successful trader. Beyond the outskirts of the city, he built a summer
mansion which he called Greenwich House. It was impressive enough to give its name to the community which became famous in the annals of American art and literature as Greenwich
Village.

Corne's second marriage, after Betsey's grandmother had died,
to the widow of his partner Isaac Van Dam, inspired him with
mounting rage and ended in a legal separation. By then he had
retired to a valuable farm near Peekskill. His stay there was interrupted by the Revolution. Corne could not resist shouting his
passionate allegiance to George III into the faces of Rebel committeemen. States had known him in London when they were
both refugees frequenting the New York Coffee House.

When a middle-aged man becomes engaged to an adolescent
girl the instantaneous assumption is that he pounced hungrily on
his blushing prey. But both States's personal past and the future
of his marriage imply that she was the prime mover. There is no
indication that the marriage had entered the perennial bachelor's
vision of contented retirement. Although kept almost certainly

within acceptable limits — Dyckman was a conventional man repelled by revolutionary behavior — his major passion had been the one that had eventuated so tragically: for his sister Caty. He was clearly an admirer of other women, but the liaison that seems to have produced issue reveals a complete lack of concern with establishing a permanent household. Some two years after they had separated, he cared enough about Eleanor Brewer and States Dyckman Brewer to put them among his principal legatees, but had lost track of their whereabouts. In London, he had found domesticity without any trammels under the non-matrimonial wing of Mrs. Tait.

Yet, whatever may be his views of his future, it is extremely difficult for a middle-aged man, susceptible to women, to be unswayed by the passionate admiration of a seductive and pure adolescent girl. States, being in his early forties, was furthermore at the queasy age when a male, fearful that he has passed his prime, is eager for the reassurance that a young love can best give.

Betsey liked to play at being more childish than she actually was. The girl's character was in fact more solid and dedicated than that of her older, more worldly admirer. States's nerves, although he was still keeping them mostly under control, tended to play him tricks, but Betsey was able to write, during a desperate crisis in 1802, that until then she had never realized she had any nerves. Her manner was extremely feminine, and she prided herself on its being so, writing after she had been openly incisive that she feared States would find her too "masqueline," a strange misspelling. Yet, within the accepted feminine sphere of which courting was a major aspect, she went throughout her life powerfully her own way.

Born in 1776, the child of Loyalists, Elizabeth was thrown at birth into difficulties. Since there was no possibility of silencing Corne, the family strategy was to keep his property in Westchester from confiscation under anti-Tory legislation by seeming to turn it over to his son-in-law, Dennis Kennedy, Betsey's father. Kennedy owned "a large, barn-like house" near Peekskill,* and had been adequately discreet to be passed off as "well-affected" to the Continental Congress. The repeated alarms caused by patriot greed for Corne's property and understandable doubts as to Kennedy's true position could not have meant anything to the infant, but she must have had to build interior defenses to continual family strain. Eventually, Corne's farm and mill were seized by the Commissioners of Sequestration and sold to an important patriot. Kennedy appealed to the Provincial Congress. Although he convinced that body of his patriotism and his right to hold the property, the Commissioners of Sequestration would not back down. The result was an argumentative correspondence — but Corne never got his property back.

Kennedy continued to walk the tightrope. In 1779, he actually achieved a commission in the Westchester militia. However, this triumph boomeranged since it raised charges that he was, in fact, "strongly connected with the enemy." (It is pleasant to suppose that he was one of the secret Loyalists who smuggled teams to States Dyckman.) Eventually Kennedy disappeared from Westchester, never, as far as we know, to return.

There now comes a long gap in Elizabeth's biography embellished only by the rumor that she was taken with other children to the cellar of a house where they were grouped before a curtain. The curtain was pulled back, revealing a picture of George III, and the children were commanded to "kneel before your master." How Elizabeth was separated from her immediate family to become in effect the daughter of her grandfather we do

---

*Elizabeth, of course, had no memory of the high Rebel officer who was brought, presumably dying, to her father's house in 1777. General Washington's aide, Lieutenant Colonel Alexander Hamilton, had been stricken on his way back from his major mission to General Horatio Gates. He was nursed for several months at Kennedy's before he could make the journey back to headquarters.

The view from Dyckman's birthplace (now near 110th Street) on Manhattan Island. He looked out over the plains of Harlem, the East River and Long Island Sound, with the western shore of Long Island beyond. Watercolor by Deputy Quartermaster General Archibald Robertson. Courtesy New York Public Library

Huge bridges now connect Manhattan with the mainland across the Harlem River. Here is Dyckman's Bridge, which States's father helped build in the 1750s. Defying aristocratic monopoly, the bridge helped bankrupt the Dyckman family.

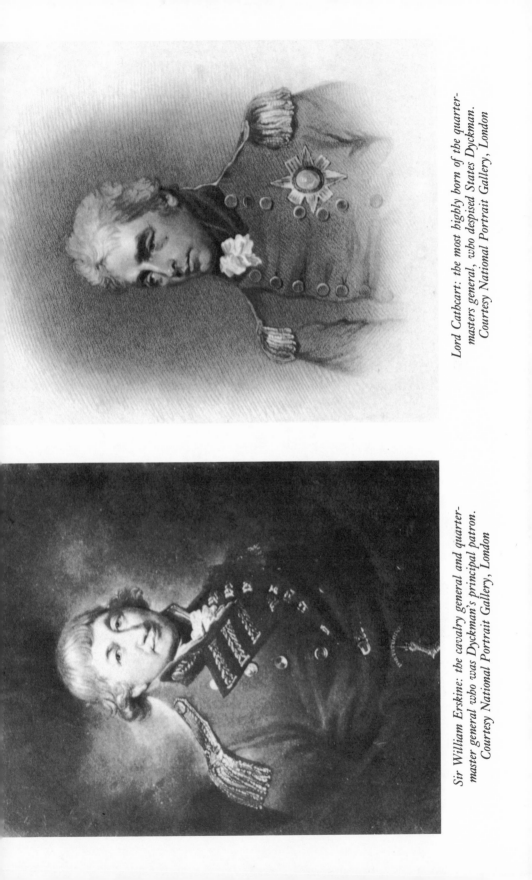

Sir William Erskine: the cavalry general and quartermaster general who was Dyckman's principal patron.
Courtesy National Portrait Gallery, London

Lord Cathcart: the most highly born of the quartermasters general, who despised States Dyckman.
Courtesy National Portrait Gallery, London

General Dalrymple: the greediest of Dyckman's quartermasters. The original caption reads: "Agamemnon A Great General. Taken on the Steyne at Brighton." Courtesy National Portrait Gallery, London

The Adelphi: the architectural triumph, designed by the brothers Adam, which stood beside Dyckman's lodgings in London, and where he often wandered.
Courtesy New York Public Library

A beauty of the Adelphi: Emma Hart, the future Lady Hamilton.
Drawn by Angelica Kauffman. Courtesy British Library

Archibald Robertson: the mildest of Dyckman's quartermasters, who, as an amateur watercolorist, drew pictures, some here reproduced, of Dyckman's world. After George Romney. Courtesy New York Public Library

Lawers: the mansion in Perthshire, which Robertson was enabled to build by his huge gains as quartermaster.
Courtesy New York Public Library

Elizabeth Corne Kennedy: the young girl Dyckman married, when he was middle-aged, over the opposition of her family.
Artist unknown. Courtesy Boscobel

*Peter Corne: the old slave trade[r]
and legalized pirate, who was
outraged by the marriage of hi[s]
granddaughter to States Dyckman. Artist unknown. Courte[sy]
Boscobel Restoration, Inc.*

*Corne Dyckman: the sickly fruit
of Dyckman's marriage. Artist
unknown. Courtesy Boscobel*

William Cobbett: the fiery controversialist, who was Dyckman's friend host and champion in London. Engraving after a painting by J. R. Smith. Courtesy National Portrait Gallery, London

Cobbett in action: the caption on this print, from the
title page of Huish's 1836 book on Cobbett, quotes the
pamphleteer, "You shall find that the serpent can
sting those who attempt to annoy him."
Courtesy New York Public Library

PALL MALL.

Wedgwood and Byerly, one of the fine stores in London where Dyckman shopped. Courtesy New York Public Library

Snuff box with a portrait of Charles II, which
Dyckman had made from the wood of the Royal
Oak. Courtesy Boscobel Restoration, Inc.

View from Peekskill looking south, June 3, 1779. Dyckman's Hudson River world as depicted by his quartermaster and patron Archibald Robertson. Courtesy New York Public Library

China by Wedgwood which Dyckman bought.
Courtesy Boscobel Restoration, Inc.

Boscobel, the manion house that was the culmination of Dyckman's career.
Photographed on its original site by Cortlandt D. Hubbard.
Courtesy Boscobel Restoration, Inc., and the photographer

not know. Her parents are never mentioned in the Dyckman Papers. It is clear that States did meet a brother, but the contact was brief and the brother disappeared into the British military service.

The girl living on a farm with a choleric old sea captain was hungry for exquisite things. What a joy to visit Dyckman's house where she could admire the elegances he had brought to the Hudson Valley! Long after she had married him, she exclaimed, "What taste you have!"

To Betsey, the new cutting edge of Dyckman's temper did not show itself. How infinitely suaver he was than the other men who entered her world! When Corne was asked about his stay as a refugee in London, he would growl and denounce, but Dyckman would describe wonderful things: fine equipages moving through the streets of a great city; how society gathered at fashionable watering places and public gardens. He could describe the costumes of beautiful aristocrats in such detail that Betsey was entranced by the vision and his memory. She fell deeply in love. Even his bouts with excruciating illness appealed to her emotions: she had a passion for taking care of those who suffered.

The Dyckman Papers contain a scribbled draft, almost illegible, of an undated letter to "My Worthy Friend," obviously Corne. The opening reveals how his ailing sister, Caty, tied States down. Despite his need to meet Corne at a dinner party, he could not go, since "Mrs. Hale" was "not yet well enough to take so long a ride." It had been his "intention of submitting a circumstance to you upon which my happiness in a great manner depends and which I flatter myself you are not totally ignorant of." The "sensibility" of his "feelings" had made him not wish to discuss the matter in Corne's house, partly because Elizabeth, of whose "approbation" he felt "assured," might be present, and

[133]

partly because "should I be unfortunate, I would not for the world" want anyone, not excluding Elizabeth's aunt, Mrs. Douglas, to know. He hoped Corne would come to his house.

"I beg a line from you if I am to be so happy —" he began, breaking off before he made clear his meaning. Referring, so it seems, to possible criticism of his wooing a girl behind her elders' backs, he wrote, "If you do not find . . . my conduct perfectly open and candid, punish me with the loss of your friendship, the greatest exception I can meet with."

Whether or not States sent his clumsily oblique avowal, an avowal was eventually made. Corne was far from pleased. No parent wishes his offspring to marry an ailing, much older man, and it was in the eighteenth century an absolute duty to investigate her suitor's finances. In answer to questioning, Dyckman dwelt heavily on his funds in England, and the obligations to him of his former employers, including a vague promise from Bruen which he did not himself really count on. Corne, who was a hard man to convince of anything, was not convinced. However, there was little the grandfather could do. Betsey had as much iron in her makeup as did the rest of her family — and she loved her man. She faced down, in addition to the old slaver and privateer, her aunt, Mrs. Douglas, whom the record reveals as among the most determined of womankind.

Perhaps to counteract Corne's skepticism, States conspicuously lavished money on his farmhouse in preparation for his bride. Patronizing, as he had in London, the best merchants and craftsmen, he bought fine chairs, card tables, and sofas from Gifford and Scotland, looking glasses from William Wilmerding, curtains and ingrain carpeting from Alexander Norwood, for a total cost of £302.13.3. King's Grange was painted and the fanlight over the door repaired. Thomas Burrow provided green paper for the walls and gilded an oval frame. But as States proceeded enthusiastically, he emptied his reservoir of funds.

Beginning in November, 1793, visitors noticed that Dyckman

no longer took them into his library to admire the effect of the volumes that rose, in varied hues of bound leather, to the very ceiling. It did not take long for the neighborhood to find out that the books were upriver at Chancellor Robert R. Livingston's mansion. Dyckman had sold all the 1,400 volumes of "London editions." Down the years he was to mourn this loss as one of the major humiliations forced on him by adverse circumstances and dishonest men.

Surely the economic implications of this disappearance were dinned into Betsey's ears by her relations. All in vain. States bought new clothes for himself, Caty, Caty's son William, and his widowed sister, Mrs. Vredenburgh. During March, 1794, at New York City's Trinity Church States Dyckman, aged forty or forty-one, was married to Elizabeth Corne Kennedy, than eighteen.

The insertion into a lifelong bachelor's household of a gentle but convinced girl, who was in effect both wife and daughter, could not but cause a revolution. Not that Betsey fought with anybody. No jealousy emerged between the two women who so loved States and were now living together under his roof: Caty was a bird with a broken wing, and Betsey nursed birds with broken wings. The wife's efficiency and devotion in taking care of her mother-in-law encouraged the invalid old lady increasingly to spend time in States's home. Betsey even achieved the miracle of endearing herself to Sill while taking the housekeeper's long-held control. Although not as quickly fecund as many a young wife, Betsey added to her entourage two babies: Peter Corne Dyckman (born January, 1797) and Letitia Catalina (June, 1799). Her husband's namesake and probably illegitimate son, States Dyckman Brewer, needing a home, Betsey gathered him in. Referring to him as "dear States," she mothered the boy, although he was only two or three years her junior. If Betsey — she never disobeyed an outright command — decided to act without asking her husband's agreement, it was always to bring into the household more gentleness and kindness and generosity.

When her husband came down with the gout, he was nursed as he had never been nursed before. The devotion of the young woman, with her strong, comfortable body was unwavering. In her amorous relationship with her husband, Betsey played the role of a kittenish child. They developed a kind of baby talk which added to any emotional word the sound "ee." They referred to each other as "dearest liffe." She confessed, with a maidenly blush, that she longed to lay her head on his "boodie."

Dyckman felt he should be very happy. He was eager to bask in the warm sunlight of conquering domesticity — but he could not. He believed himself much in love with his wife and very fortunate in his marriage, yet old wounds which he had hoped to close forever were reopened.

The whole thrust of his new life was centripetal, towards the family hearth. He may have remained a bachelor for so long because the hearth of his childhood had, as he was torn from place to place by his father's ever recurring money troubles, betrayed him. He was reminded of how he had then been humiliated before the world every time he stepped into the room where his library had been and saw the nakedness of the walls that was hardly softened by the imported prints he had hung there. This new humiliation was intimately connected with his marriage. It had resulted from expenditures spurred by his desire to impress his bride and her relations. But his maneuver had boomeranged, increasing the relations' distrust.

Betsey's lack of concern with his financial affairs — she would not even listen to his explanations — indicated on her part complete trust. Yet her presence in his life and the environment she had created around him, and his love for her had reduced his maneuverability. The fact was that a sinister wobble was menacing the entire stability of his financial position. His own hearth might soon be as unstable as his father's had been. And he knew that his wife's family was watching, gleeful, so it seemed to him, in their anticipation of a downfall which would prove that they had been prescient in scorning him and disapproving of the match.

On the fourteenth of October, 1794, some seven months after his marriage to Betsey, States sent the following letter to his grandfather-in-law: "Sir, There is a mare, a colt and two hogs belonging to you upon my farm. Was I to follow the impulse of my own feelings I would immediately turn them out upon the public road, but that such a measure would inevitably lead to a discovery of too much of your conduct for the happiness and peace of mind of my wife. In order therefore to keep her if possible from the knowledge of your imperious behavior towards me (which by the by has excited only my contempt) I have enclosed you 100 dollars which I believe will be acknowledged the full value of the colt and hogs. The mare shall be at Jonathan Odell's next Saturday.

"I have also enclosed you 50 dollars for the *outfit* you gave your grandchild upon her marriage. Should I have underrated the things a few shillings which I can hardly suppose, I am willing to conclude our correspondence and connection by paying the balance. Were it not for the reasons above given (the regard I have for your child's tranquility) I would put the things in a band box and return them to you — S M D."

At the close of 1796, more than five years after Caty's addiction had been discovered, it was decided to test whether she were now ready to go somewhat out into the world. She rented a room in the village of Harlem from a McGown cousin.* Hale intervened. Leaving her loose and unchaperoned was, he insisted,

---

* Her landlord was the son of the Mrs. McGown who had taken over the Black Horse Tavern and whose curse had immediately preceded the fatal fall from his horse of States's and Caty's father.

not "proper or decent." He was determined to drive her back into seclusion in States's house. According to States, his object was to support his assertion, delivered always with maximum self-pity, that, though the most loving of husbands, he could not bring his wife home since her condition "rendered retirement necessary."

Through his lawyer, Hoffman, Hale threatened McGown with prosecution of harboring a wife without the husband's permission. McGown was frightened, but a braver cousin took Caty in. Hale then appeared at Harlem and "went through the whole village" forbidding Caty's relations to receive her. This done, he joined other passengers on the stage to Tarrytown. As the stage awaited its departure time, Hale was informed that he was wanted outside.

Benjamin, States, and William Dyckman had galloped to their sister's defense. However, States was so emotionally upset that Hale found awaiting him at the exit from the stagecoach only the other two brothers. They were both burly farmers and their faces were working with fury. On seeing them, Hale "appeared ready from terror to throw himself at their feet." When William stated that "I was determined to protect her . . . even at the risk of my life against the insults of you or anyone who dare attempt it," Hale replied pacifically that he "believed it, and thought she had reason to be thankful to me for it."

The brothers demanded that Hale specify the evidence which Hoffman had stated "would entitle him to divorce." Hale tried to appease the hostile faces and clenched fists by avowing "he wished to his soul" that he had not inspired Hoffman's letter. Under present circumstances, it did not seem prudent to repeat what he had been told by Negroes and a servant girl whose own virtue had been impugned. "He acknowledged that he had no evidence but of her general bad temper and her taking laudanum; that he had no doubt of her fidelity." Then with a sudden burst of spirit, he added, "There were other means of obtaining divorce."

The brothers told him to go ahead. If he did not "either bring on action or . . . do her justice in another way," they would persuade her to bring suit against him, thus exposing his effort to justify his "cruelty" and "barbarity" by aspersing "the character of his wife."

When the brothers questioned his behavior at Harlem, the terrified husband offered to beg McGown to take Caty back. He would apologize to the other cousins, and instruct his lawyer never again to interfere with her activities.

This account of the confrontation, which comes altogether from Dyckman sources, is given credence by what we know of Hale's character, and more specifically, by a note preserved in the Dyckman Papers, dated January 18, 1797, scribbled on scratch paper in Hale's handwriting, and addressed to Hoffman: "Since speaking to you, I have conversed with Messrs. William and Benjamin Dyckman on the subject of Mrs. Hale's situation, and I have agreed with them that Mrs. Hale is to remain under their direction, and they are to determine whether she is to stay at McGown's at Harlem or with them or in any situation with which they may be satisfied."

This paper in their hands, the brothers allowed Hale to escape back into the stage and set off with it to Tarrytown. But once he was out of their reach, his determination revived.

The opening gun of the new campaign was a letter to States from Hale's sister. "You know that before you returned home to this country she was comfortably settled with her husband and children, and that I myself often told you that taking her so often about, away from her family, would not end well. . . . I believe you will agree with me that if you had not interfered with her, things would not have gone as they have." He could not now evade the responsibility "to save her from every slander" by carrying her back into his home. How would States feel "when you came to your death bed and reflect that you have left your sister to be exposed to so many dangers?"

Hale directed his own letters to States's brothers. One included charges against States that elicited from him an affidavit (lost) in which (as he admitted without specifying further) he had been forced, in order to defend Caty's character, to impeach his own morals. States penned a seemingly endless emotional and repetitious epistle to two leading citizens of Albany in order to inform public opinion there of the iniquity of Hale.

The two brothers acted more decisively. On receipt of a letter from Hale repeating "the long stories our family has repeatedly been troubled with," and threatening to seek a divorce, this time in Connecticut, William wrote, "If you intended to insult me why did you not do it when we met at Harlem, and show yourself a little more a man of spirit?" If he ever again heard Hale's "pitiful falsehoods" against Caty, "I shall be under the necessity of demanding such satisfaction as none but a coward will refuse to give." Benjamin endorsed William's communication, adding, "After our meeting at Harlem, when you had an opportunity of stating what you pleased, I was in hopes we should be no more troubled with you."

These letters, sent on February 28, 1797, so frightened their recipient — the man who claimed to have been a major in the Continental Army clearly had no taste for the smell of gunpowder — that they are the last documents in the Dyckman Papers dealing with Hale.* There was no divorce. On April 22, his friend George Pollock wrote States, "I am happy to find Mrs.

---

*Hale, who died on September 2, 1821, prospered in Albany. Some years after his enemy, States Dyckman, had been memorialized by the erection of Boscobel, Hale erected a "mansion" on Pearl Street, selecting a strange way to make it memorialize himself. When the building was torn down in 1860, four copper plates were found embedded in the walls. Three inches long and two wide, they bore "in Roman letters" the inscription, "Daniel Hale, 1813."

Hale is settling for the present in Harlem, and will do all in my power to contribute to her happiness and comfort."

Caty had won her freedom. She was no longer an albatross around her brother's neck, and States's home was exorcised of the malign spirit of Hale. But other horrors walked.

CHAPTER THIRTEEN

⤚∾⤙

A Waking Nightmare

HAVING, so it seemed forever, abandoned the quartermaster's business, Dyckman had revealed no intentions of wandering again on such elevated and slippery paths, or, indeed, of making any further use of his gifts for advancing himself. Now operating privately in his own world, he had no recourse to the equivocal financial expedients which were accepted by British officialdom as essential to the game they all were required by social necessity to play. However, he applied to his personal behavior the British conception, so different from the mores of his native America, that a gentleman does not engage in trade. His purchasing and selling of local farmland would have been considered entirely suitable to a British landowner — and he operated on a small scale, making no great profits. His object was to live in his retirement on what he had already earned.

Dyckman had left behind in London more than £2,000 to be invested by his bankers, John and George Whitehead. The interest plus his £100 annual annuity from Sir William Erskine could be counted on to support him in the Hudson Valley as a conspicuously well-fixed farmer, surrounded with objects of taste already paid for, who did not farm too seriously. However, his recurring funds could achieve little more. And he realized that to invade his capital would overset all. Conscious of his drive towards extravagance, he swore that he would never invade his capital. Yet he had hardly reached America before he began making drafts on the Whiteheads.

Looking back, he liked to blame what had happened on his generosity in succoring numerous impoverished relatives. In supporting this excuse, he was forced to exaggerate. He had, it is true, been generous, but his brothers, particularly the prosperous Benjamin, had helped to alleviate needs within their tight family circle. States had, in fact, done what he resolved not to do: he had dribbled away his funds through improvident purchases.

Only five years after his return to America, the climactic moment came. On February 11, 1792, Dyckman ordered the Whiteheads to sell all his remaining securities they held for him (by then worth only £472). On the very day that he dispatched this order, he bought locally table luxuries at a cost of £14.2.6. Two months later, he wiped out his capital in America by selling for $2,400 his New York State stock.

States's behavior by no means signaled that he had overcome the terror, descended from childhood experiences, of public financial disgrace. That was an obsessive foreboding walking wakeful nights. Practiced bit by bit in daylight, "lack of economy" (as he called it) was an addiction for which temptation was perpetual. And, like many another addiction, it could seem to assuage the greater fear. How could he, while making agreeable expensive purchases which impressed his neighbors, regard himself as financially straitened?

Seven months after his marriage, States was forced to sell King's Grange, which he had so expensively fixed up to receive his young bride. His friends the New York merchants Carlisle and George Pollock agreed to $15,000, $3,000 down and the rest to be paid at intervals. Since the Pollocks bought the farm for resale, the Dyckmans could temporarily stay on, although no longer in their own house. In less than a year, one Davenish signed for King's Grange. States took his family to a farm he acrimoniously bought from his brother William — a move made more unpleasant because it entailed displacing, to some family outrage, his widowed sister, Mrs. Vredenburgh. He left behind the furniture he had acquired for his marriage. Davenish had agreed to pay for it what States said he had himself paid, £302.13.3.

But Davenish was short of money. King's Grange remained unoccupied. Every time Dyckman passed, he saw the agricultural improvements he had achieved running to ruin. If he peered through the windows he could observe the furniture he so loved gathering dust. Finally, Pollock urged him to the rescue: "I know what you once made the farm and that no one is more capable of restoring it." However, Pollock saw nothing to be gained by suing Davenish for the price of the furniture.

Davenish disappeared. One Brotherson bought King's Grange. Unimpressed with Dyckman's furniture, he insisted that it was not worth more than £200. The London-experienced connoisseur was humiliated by having a New York upholsterer come in for an appraisal. States would only allow some pieces to go at what he considered a humiliating price.

Dyckman was still spending money, if not as lavishly as before, imprudently. During May, 1795, he hired a sloop and took Betsey, Caty with her son William, and Mrs. Vredenburgh on a fourteen-day excursion upriver. They supped at Clermont where States saw distinctive bindings he had once owned sandwiched between alien volumes in Chancellor Livingston's library. He discussed with the experimental farmer the value of plaster of Paris for enriching the soil. The "jaunt" cost £20.13.10.

The Erskine annuity, on which what remained of the Dyckman prosperity depended, came in irregularly — and then came in not at all. Early in 1794, on the eve of his own marriage,

States had finally found the fortitude to write directly to his former intimate patron. The letter was designed, at the sacrifice of facts, to appeal to emotions.

States wrote that he had intended, after a short "visit" to America, to pass "the remainder of my days in England." He would then have been able to share in, or at least witness, "the honor you have been reaping in the favor of your country contending for religion against infidelity." (States had heard that Erskine. was commanding in Flanders the English cavalry in the allied army fighting the atheistic forces of the French Revolution.) Dyckman attributed his stay in America to the dependence on him of his relations.

Dyckman would not "enter into detail of all the troubles, disappointments, and misfortunes I have experienced since the happy days I passed with you or under your protection," since if Erskine retained "any part of the friendship I was so honored with," he would find the account too distressing. It was "absolutely necessary" that Dyckman receive every six months the £50 to which he was entitled. "It is not my business to complain, but had you or C.B. [Colonel Bruen] answered the first letters I wrote you on my arrival here, I should not have felt the hand of affliction so heavy. I hope, however, my misfortune so far from depriving me utterly of your friendship will recall the favorable sentiments you once felt for me and which, I venture to assert, I have by no action of my life forfeited.

"Believe me, with the sincerest attachment . . ."

Dyckman refused to "allow myself to think" that Erskine would not respond to this appeal. Yet month after month ships sailed in from England, and there was no reply. After more than a year had passed, in March, 1795, States wrote, with profuse apologies, to Mrs. Erskine. He begged her to get in touch for him with her husband. His own bankers had refused to accept the last bill he had drawn on Erskine. He feared it would come back "protested," subjecting him to considerable expense.*

That fall, he heard from the Whiteheads that Erskine had died in the spring. The bankers, having received no payment, were trying to contact the heir, Sir William, Jr. Trying to reactivate, for the beginning at least on a small scale, Bruen's verbal promise of £200 a year "till the account should be finally settled," States drew on Bruen for £100. This effort disappeared into silence. His balance in London totaled £17.

Erskine, Jr., proved no more willing to answer communications than had his father. At the Whiteheads' urging, Dyckman demonstrated that he was really alive by procuring an affidavit from the mayor of New York, Richard Varick, witnessed by Alexander Hamilton's intimate, Robert Troup.

By the Christmas of 1795 no one would accept Dyckman's drafts on the Erskines at however high a discount. Obviously intending to pass on the costs, Dyckman began borrowing the exact equivalent of the annuity — £50 every six months — at the high interest rate of short loans: 2½ percent a month. No payments arriving from abroad, he continued his borrowing until the compounded interest was almost equal to the money he had received.

States was now identifying himself on deeds as "farmer." His activity is indicated by numerous accounts and bills, the most piquant item to an uninformed eye being a blacksmith's charge of one shilling for "upsetting a stubborn hoe." Like his father before him, States could not resist expansive public gestures. His neighbors contributed between 5 and 250 dollars each towards mending the road from Peekskill to Croton Ferry. States contributed $350.

Betsey, although worried by their financial state — "the tax man and Wolford will bring me to poverty" — was as girlishly loving as ever: "It is thirty-two long hours since I saw you. It

---

*Penalties, fees, and difficulties of international exchange added, according to States, 20 percent to the cost of redeeming in America a bill protested in England.

will be at least as many more before I see you again, but I keep up my spirits as well as I can. . . . I am just going to bed. To-night and tomorrow night I will dream of laying my head on my dear boodie. The next night I will lay there in reality."

Dyckman's gout was flourishing on his nervous strain. He was visited by fevers. He was finding it unbearable to await help-lessly, at a distance of three thousand miles, for answers which never came. He frightened Betsey by shouting that he would have to go to England and fight the battle there. Nineteen months to the day after he had written his piteous appeal to the elder Erskine, on October 10, 1796, he wrote angrily to the younger: "You will not be surprised at my declaring that my pa-tience is nearly exhausted." Unless on receipt of this letter the annuity was liquidated for £1,000 plus all costs and arrears, Dyckman would set out for England. "In that event, you must certainly consider yourself responsible for the additional expense."

This threat was obviously feeble: Dyckman burst into an-other. "Indeed, the total neglect by which I have been treated by Colonel Bruen, as well as the other gent. of the QMC Dep. in the late American War, whose fortunes I have very much con-tributed to, has been such as would justify me was I to make use of this power I possess of reminding those concerned of how much I have been their friend, and how much it has been to their interest I should continue so. As I was sent out here by Colonel Bruen upon a private business of the late department, it was necessary to bring with me sundry private papers which will abundantly prove what I have said."

In addition to the implication of public exposure, this letter contained what was in the world to which it was dispatched an unpardonable contention. In protecting the exalted quartermas-ters, States had been not a subordinate but a "friend." He did, later in the letter, refer to himself as a "faithful servant," but even this sentence — "It is the privilege of the aggrieved to complain and the duty of the fortunate to do justice to faithful servants" — did not come out right. Dyckman had characterized the aristocrats not as innately superior but "fortunate"; he had demanded not bounty but "justice"; and he had lectured his betters on their duty. Years in the equalitarian United States had changed the returned Loyalist.

When, after his return to America, Bruen and the senior Erskine had not answered his letters, Dyckman did not press to keep any of the old relationships alive, nor did he remain in touch with how the quartermaster investigations were faring. After his financial troubles had struck, he blamed his difficulties on the "contemptuous indifference" of his former patrons. Strangely, he restricted his calls for help to the Erskines who were legally in his debt and Bruen whom he could remind of promises. Why, in particular, did he not appeal to Robertson, whose pocketbook had always opened to him at the asking? Was he, as "a friend," ashamed to beg like a servant? Revulsion against his obsequiousness in London had helped to make him into one of the proudest — if very uneasily proud — of men.

Dyckman's pride became most grievously wounded by his relationship with his wife's family. The weakness of his financial situation, which had been the main reason for their opposing, to his outrage, his marriage, was now drawing him, as currents pull a disabled ship against reefs, into dependence on their condescension. The Cornes were, as his own family were not, rich. Although he had become related to them against their wills, they could not allow Betsey and her children to sink into penury. They were Dyckman's last resource, but there was nothing he less desired in life than to be forced to ask for what they would surely point out was charity, unwillingly granted.

Through the purchase of William's farm, States had become a

next-door neighbor to Corne, a proximity that did not make things easier. As the result of some unrecorded unpleasantness, Corne ordered States to keep out of his house. States frowned on his wife's visiting where he was barred, but how could Betsey refrain from traversing with her offspring the few hundred yards between her home and that of the grandfather by whom she had been raised?

Eventually, States wrote, "Respected Sir: Unfortunately lying under your displeasure, the obtrusion of a letter will doubtless occasion some surprise, but as it is dictated by a heart influenced by no unworthy motives, your candor will at least pardon it." States acknowledged "an error. . . . Did I not stand more in fear of an envious and selfish world than I do of the construction you would place upon it, my acknowledgments should be as explicit as you wish. Convinced, as I am persuaded you are, that interested motives do not actuate me, you will have the goodness to attribute this solely to the desire I have of restoring peace to the bosom of a beloved wife and consequently happiness to my own."

The plea seems to have been successful but the uneasiness which induced States to insist twice on his lack of interested motives, could not be dispelled. It was darkened by an unforeseeable catastrophe. Dyckman's financial ship, if listing and leaky, was still afloat, when, in what promised to be the safest channel he had opened, it struck a reef. The Pollocks, through disappointments experienced in their West Indian trade, were unable to meet a payment on their purchase of King's Grange. Dyckman was forced to seek financial aid from one of his wife's relations. He borrowed $3,000 from George Douglas, who had married Betsey's aunt. How the wife gloated!

The former Margaret Corne was almost incredibly disagreeable and self-willed. She was to sentence one of her daughters to eternal spinsterhood because no suitor seemed to her rich enough. When another daughter became engaged to James

Monroe, the favorite nephew of the then President of the United States, she tried to block the match because the Virginian would not agree never to take his wife and potential children away from New York. "I could never think," Mrs. Douglas explained, "of her living any place where I cannot see them daily." The third daughter ran wild. A disciple of Mme. de Staël, she became adequately notorious in both America and England as "the American Corinne" to become the subject of a modern biography.

Dyckman got on with George Douglas, who was an extremely prosperous Scottish merchant, agreeably on a business basis, but Douglas died in 1799 and Dyckman's debt came into the widow's hands. States was to write Betsey that the treatment he received from her grandfather, "as the acts of age and a temper never the happiest, I could for your sake have borne . . . but the purse-proud Mrs. Douglas, who told you she was the only member of the family who had married above a beggar — to be in the power of such a narrow-hearted contracted being was a matter too humiliating for your husband."

Everything was going wrong as if the curse, which had preceded his father's death, were being applied to the son. In a lawsuit, he lost valuable property because of an unsuspected flaw in the title. Even good news boomeranged. He was jubilant at a report that Erskine, Jr., had agreed to buy up the annuity and pay arrears: £1,300. With a draft on Erskine for that amount, he liquidated the debt he had contracted in £50 installments, and collected some expendable cash. But Erskine did not bother to acknowledge the existence of the draft, which lay month after month with Dyckman's London bankers, running up extra costs.

For the second time in four years, Dyckman had conspicuously to downgrade himself and his family by moving into inferior quarters. As he had sold King's Grange, he now sold his home, the sawmill, the stream, the woodlot and the river landing. On November 23, 1798, crowds trampled in to bid for Dyckman's "excellent milch cows, young cattle (amongst them several English bull and heifer calves), sheep, hog, horses, and colts. Also a quantity of the best fresh and salt hay, and sundry other articles, together with half a field of excellent green wheat." The voice of the auctioneer may well have carried to the Corne house nearby.

The property to which Dyckman moved his family was worth a quarter of that he had just sold. He was now a dirt farmer like his humbler neighbors, trying to make every cent he could from unlovely utilitarian acres. Almost all the objects of virtue he had brought back from London or bought in the United States were gone. But out of the squalor, the shame, the sense of persecution, there rose a dream, which, in the face of all misfortunes, he was incredibly, at long last, to bring true. On July 9, 1798, George Pollock wrote the almost bankrupt farmer, "I long to walk over the point with you and find the site for your future mansion house."

Dyckman felt a passionate need to reclaim "that estimation in society which I now lose by having it known I am indebted to sundry persons without the *immediate* ability to pay." He had seen too much of the world not to be conscious of ways by which a clever man could gain, without too much risk of exposure, large sums through taking advantage of others. However, there is no record that he ever in the United States played a sharper's game. He wished at home to stand as a shining example of rectitude. Thus the only escape that was left to him from the public humiliation of being clearly in financial trouble was privately to humiliate himself before his wife's family. He brought himself to ask Corne to enable him to consolidate his debts by lending him £1,500 as mortgage on his remaining farm. When Corne, having expressed "reluctance" at being "obliged" thus to invest his money, wished to handle the transaction in a way that would make the farm altogether Betsey's property, States responded with a scorching and horrifying scream of wounded pride. He had not answered sooner, he explained, because his wife had been "so indisposed of late that I have not been able to tranquilize my mind sufficiently to write upon a subject so painful. . . . As soon as I can leave my wife," he would hurry to New York "and make inquiries for a good vessel to England where I hope to meet with some friends, unless they are much changed by my change."

Friends in England! A communication had finally been extorted from Erskine, Jr., who denied ever having heard of the situation before. He wished Dyckman to be informed "that I am most sincerely concerned he should have suffered any inconvenience on my account." He would pay off the bond with interest "as soon as I can. I am sorry it will not be in my power to do it immediately as I have very large sums to pay at this term. I hope Mr. Dyckman will not think of putting himself to the trouble for coming to England." States's representatives, who were George Douglas's British partners, also wrote that it would do no good for him to come. They saw little prospect of securing the money soon.

Betsey wrote her husband, "You are no doubt now in New York and I hope well and in better spirits than when you left me. I had my fortune told yesterday and was told that all will be well, and I am disposed to believe it."

Dyckman was indeed in a dreadful state of mind. He had not been enabled to quiet his local creditors. Crying out against "the mortifying, the deadly sting of poverty," he concluded that the neighbors were beginning "to shun us as an infection." "Your relations," he shouted to Betsey, "as well as my unworthy set, were the first to cast us off." When one of his brothers was referred to, he answered angrily that he had no brothers.

It was his early terror all over again, but worse. He was not now a stricken child, but the individual whose extravagance (as he could not deny) had torn away his family's armor against the hammer blows of circumstance. That these blows came on so thickly, so relentlessly, and so inexplicably, added a sense of persecution, of fear. He darkly foresaw being carried away to debtors' prison.

Under a humiliation greater than he could bear, suspecting everyone he met of sneers or condescension, forever waiting for good news only to have every dispatch from England sink him deeper, States believed himself on the verge of insanity. He felt that to "linger" even one year longer would carry him "with a broken heart" to a "cold grave." In the grave he could forget, he told Betsey, "the chilling hand of charity extended by your cold-hearted relations." If he stayed in America, he had no resource except to "retire from my own painful feelings" into the grave.

Although he had been assured that he could accomplish nothing by crossing the ocean, at least he could act rather than just wait helplessly. He could confront and perhaps defeat those he had come to consider his enemies. He must, he told Betsey, seek in England "emancipation from the toils in which I struggled and the tyranny of those relations."

Betsey so loved her man that she accepted, if sadly, his railing against her relations. She would have liked to go along if he sailed, but she had just borne a new baby and, in any case, there was no money. She was afraid of being left lonely, afraid of all the responsibilities she would have to assume in the absence of her "dear liffe." How long an absence? Crossing the ocean could take months and, although he promised to be back in a year, his business was hardly likely to be solved so soon. Deprived of her nursing, would the sick man live to come home? But she realized that, even if their financial plight were not as desperate as he envisioned it, his state of mind left no choice. After he was gone, she wrote him that she hoped on his return "I may once more see your brow unclouded with care. In that hope and no other was I persuaded to part with you."

Betsey's family made his departure possible. Mrs. Douglas did not press for immediate payment, and Corne lent Dyckman $4,000. The security was the Dyckman farm, which was not worth that much, and the question of how the mortgage would be drawn — whether States's pride was to be hurt by specific protection for Betsey — was conveniently shelved to be settled, after States's departure, between the grandfather and the loyal wife.

On July 10, 1800, States Dyckman sailed on the *Three Sisters*. He might well need the letters — from Robert R. Livingston, John Jay, Gouverneur Morris — he had secured recommending him to the American minister in London. The quartermasters and their heirs were powerful and unlikely to be pleased by the appearance of a former employee breathing threats. Since he had used most of the money he had borrowed in order to get away, if he did not quickly extract funds from where they had previously been unextractable, he could find himself penniless in a strange city. His "reason," as he himself admitted, was "almost deranged." And his gout might strike him at any hour so that he could not move. It could kill him among strangers. Had he forgotten the man so killed, whose body had been abandoned to the ocean when he had sailed for home the other way?

"Adieu my amiable wife. Adieu my darling children. Dear Corne [his son] forget not dear Pa. And sweet Betsey, remember." He signed himself "Liffe." He was off, propelled by the foolhardy courage of despair.

∽

CHAPTER FOURTEEN

Voyage of Despair

As the *Three Sisters* moved down New York Harbor with a following breeze which he imagined, so he wrote Betsey, blew as a kind friend directly "from *our* (may I not say from *our?*) farm," Dyckman confided, "My heart is much relieved by the long delayed jaunt being at last begun." Stowed below decks were the papers which were to be, if all else failed, his philosopher's stone. Ready to threaten his former associates with the possibility of their publication, returning to a situation in which deception might again be the key to prosperity, Dyckman felt impelled to write his wife, "I have during my life been just to all men, kind and generous to my friends and affectionate to my relations. . . . I will teach our sweet boy integrity and uprightness. He shall resemble his father in all things but his want of economy." States hoped that when he and Betsey met again they would both have "done as we would wish to be done by."

After a voyage of about six weeks, Dyckman arrived at London in mid-July. He fired off a letter to Erskine, Jr.: "It can afford you little surprise and I fear as little pleasure that I am again in this country." Erskine would, of course, be responsible for the expenses of his trip. He rehearsed his grievances. "I entreat permission to wait upon you in Scotland." He would then, "if at all necessary," describe his services to Erskine's father. "Had what had taken place been proper to have been trusted in correspondence," he added ominously, "I am persuaded I need not have crossed the ocean." He had an immediate need of £200.

Dyckman assumed that since he was now within striking distance Erskine would cease to ignore him. But, as the weeks passed, he was in his old, infuriating situation: no letter. Mrs. Tait's boardinghouse had gone out of existence, yet he tried to fight strangeness by returning to the Adelphi, staying at Osborne's Hotel.

He spent more than twenty-one pounds at a fashionable tailor's: "A superfine olive Spanish coat surtout . . . A pair of superfine dark mixed color pantaloons with silk braid in the seams," etc. Although the shallow funds he had brought with him were draining away it would be a disaster for him to approach his former clients looking shabby. "It is," he explained in a letter to Betsey, "only to the fortunate that the great are liberal."

However fine the appearance he presented, "the great" would undoubtedly have been far from liberal had it not been for circumstances which Dyckman had not known when he launched on his desperate voyage: the investigations in which he had, years before, played an active part were still active. Had the issues been, as it would seem they would certainly have been, long since dead and buried, his threats of exposure would have had a hollow sound: who cares about the obsolete ravings of a former servant? He would, furthermore, have found no gainful employment to replenish his funds. The old "friendships" on which he had relied were not in their essence sound. Bruen and the elder Erskine, the patrons to whom he had been personally close, were both dead. Neither their heirs nor the surviving quartermasters were likely to be inspired to generosity by the reappearance, after so long, of a useless man with an outstretched hand. He could have been utterly ignored. Perhaps, gout having its nervous component and his emotions being so inflamed, he would have died far from home. And had he got home, it would

have been to poverty which he had dreaded, even in anticipation, to the point of paranoia.

The investigations which had continued in fits and starts during the years of Dyckman's absence had not, he discovered, in
their fundamentals changed. The accounts from the period of
the first two quartermasters, Erskine and Cathcart, still lay buried where Dyckman had done so much to bury them. General Dalrymple's period of quartermastership was under active
scrutiny.

The basic issue remained the fact that the quartermasters had
hired the wagons from themselves. Before Dyckman had arrived,
the Commissioners had come to a harsh ruling: Dalrymple and
his associates should be allowed no reimbursement for their dubious transactions: they owed the Crown all that they had received for the wagon train: £341,541.

Dalrymple screamed to his friends in Parliament against the
"injustice." That body voted that "suitable allowances" be made
for the hire and upkeep of the train. The Commissioners took
the papers back for restudy. However, Dalrymple's parliamentary connections were, in Dyckman's absence, not supplemented
by any contact with the Commissioners. He could neither find
out what they were concluding nor influence their deliberations.

Dyckman's reappearance in London seemed to Dalrymple a
godsend. Although always excitable, the general had been, when
States had last seen him, sleek and self-satisfied. Threatened year
after year with financial destruction, moored to London by his
anxiety and fear, he had become fatter and fatter. A mass of
quivering nerves, he begged Dyckman to find out and intervene.

Fortunately, the present inspector general was an old friend.
But the news he gave was not fortunate for Dalrymple. His debt
to the Crown had been cut, but only to £200,000, which would,
Dyckman commented, have "reduced" the general "to nothing."

(Accepting the Commissioners' estimate that the cost of hire
had been £341,541, and applying to this amount Dyckman's

secret admission that the profit had been at least 75 percent, sets the profit at about £56,156 more than the £200,000 the general was being asked to return. But Dalrymple had spent much during the twenty years since the money had come in.)

The unfortunate report had gone to the Lords of the Treasury, but the inspector general confided to Dyckman how it could be extracted from that labyrinthine department and returned to the Commissioners. Dalrymple could not thank Dyckman too effusively.

When Dyckman brought up his own financial plight the general's enthusiasm cooled. Now it was the wiry American who boiled. He expressed rage and bitterness, breathed threats. The rotund general tried to be soothing. He would reward Dyckman handsomely, if matters could be so arranged that he would not be ruined, but at present he had to hoard every penny. This Dyckman could not deny, yet he continued to shout about his immediate need for money. Dalrymple offered help in collecting from the others.

Dyckman intended no effort to milk Lord Cathcart, who had risen to great power in the realm and had always treated States as a clerk trying to get above himself. Although Sherriff's services as deputy quartermaster had been limited to the period for which the accounts had been passed, Dyckman called at once on his former friend. Sherriff received him with "politeness and attention," but at the mention of money became "unfeeling and unjust." The other two deputies, Bruen and Robertson, had served not only under Erskine and Cathcart but also under Dalrymple. Their profits from the earlier period had been passed, assuring a great income. But their later accounts were involved with Dalrymple's. Both rich and vulnerable, their situation created for States an obvious source of income.

Dalrymple enlisted for Dyckman a tremendously valuable ally. William Adam was Dalrymple's lawyer and also a cousin and close friend to Robertson. After a somewhat tempestuous young manhood, during which he tried to kill Charles James Fox in a duel, Adam had become a disciple of Fox's and had achieved a reputation so high that it seemed almost miraculous in the warring world where Dyckman moved. He was, in Dalrymple's words, "famed for integrity." Sir Walter Scott considered Adam "the most pleasant, kind-hearted, and benevolent man I have ever known . . . quiet, honorable, and generous."

States was ushered into the presence of a tall, robust Scot with a large oval head. His forehead occupied almost half his face, its smoothness accentuating the deeply sculptured features below: eyebrows bristling out over deepset eyes, a powerful nose with high thin nostrils, a full mouth beneath a narrow upper lip, and a bony, circular chin. The total effect was handsome. Adam's expression belied the strength of his face, being mild, competent, moody.

In his letter of introduction, Dalrymple had argued that Adam, as a one-time friend of the former Sir William Erskine, should intercede with the son: "The transactions will not endure the light and ought to be done away with both in respect of his father's honor and this gentleman's [Dyckman's] own probity. I am sure you will think so on hearing Mr. Dyckman's narration and looking at his vouchers." But Dalrymple added a warning. Dyckman's "knowledge of the business is correct as far as accounts are in question." He knew "all the rules and regulations of the office. . . . The state of the expenditure he can form a pretty valuable judgment of, but anything that relates to the connection of persons he is, I believe, ignorant of." Indeed, "he was never *confidentially* employed, being almost constantly in London [during Dalrymple's tenure], so that *he must not be informed in every particular*."

After Dyckman had expatiated on his economic plight, Adam agreed to help him at no charge. The attractive and clearly tortured stranger appealed to the considerate gentleman's compassion. The powerful Scot behaved as Dyckman's true friend.

Since Adam was recognized as the soul of probity, his support of Dyckman reveals much. Although, as Dyckman was later to state, Adam was kept ignorant of how much more the quartermasters sought (and achieved) "than we have a right to claim," Adam knew the kind of thing Dyckman was doing. As Dalrymple's lawyer, Adam was openly defending official prerogative on an extreme scale. Furthermore, he agreed that Dyckman was justified in seeking a second round of large payments. He took in his stride Dyckman's threats to use as a last resort public exposure, either through the newspapers or the law courts. This did not mean that Adam would have approved had Dyckman moved beyond threat into action. The knowledge of the practices of highly placed officials was the business of no one beyond the circle where such amenities were understood. Indeed, wide dissemination to the populace might, particularly in those days of the French Revolution, stir up serious trouble.

Adam himself wrote to Erskine, Jr. This communication from a man he dared not ignore threw the baronet into an immediate answer and profuse apologies. "I do not know how to express to you how strongly I feel the distressed situation Mr. Dyckman had been thrown into (I trust you know so much of my heart) I need not say totally from ignorance on my part. . . . The impression Mr. Dyckman must have of my conduct from the misunderstanding that has taken place in this business must be such as I trust I do not nor will ever deserve. . . . I can assure you no occurrence in my life ever hurt me more. . . . I have the greatest regard for Mr. Dyckman as I know he was of infinite service to my father who always spoke of him in the highest terms." Erskine would "willingly do everything in my power that may conduce to his convenience. . . . I shall be extremely happy to see Mr. Dyckman in Scotland and assure him personally how seriously I feel and lament." And so on. He was honoring Dyckman's request for £200.

Held in London by Dalrymple's business, Dyckman could not, for the time being, get to Scotland and Erskine, or to the Bruen family in Ireland. Perhaps Bruen had explained to his heirs that Dyckman was responsible for their wealth, and had begged his survivors to make sure that their benefactor should never want. In that case, a letter of appeal would suffice. However, Dyckman was horrified to be told that, far from dying in an open-handed mood, Bruen had ended as "a miserable miser." The appeal would have to be postponed.

But, of course, there was Robertson, dear old Robertson, who had always been so sympathetic and generous. Dyckman confidently wrote Robertson explaining his immediate need for cash. When Robertson answered with a warning that he should not be too precipitous in his demands, Dyckman cried out, "What in God's name will become of me?" He was in "a dreadful situation," haunted by "the fiend poverty." Yet, when the £200 Erskine had promised came in, Dyckman spent a large part on finery for his wife. Betsey was to respond, "Never in my life did I see anything so elegant! . . . Oh, me dear liffe, what taste you have! I am sure there never was anything so beautiful in New York as the muslins, the [illegible], and everything you sent."

In the sending, States had explained that "exclusive of the happiness I have in contributing to yours, I have another reason. It is simply this. I do not wish that your malicious neighbors or even an *acquaintance* in town should trace in your appearance too plainly the cause of my leaving you. Therefore, I wish you not only to have those presents to show but to wear."

In London, Dyckman was subject to fits of hysteria which he himself found terrifying. Expatiating on financial needs, he wrote, "My mind is and has been for three days such a [illegible] of distraction . . . that I know not if I express myself intelligibly but this I know, that no language can express the feelings." At about the same date, Dalrymple tried to cool him down as a negotiator: "I fancy on Friday you will be more successful, you showing your usual caution and indifference."

During September, when the Commissioners went on vacation, States finally set off on the mission for which he had crossed the ocean: to confront his patron's son on whom he had for so many years concentrated his thoughts, anticipations, disappointments, curses.

This Sir William Erskine haunted the indefinable borderland between eccentricity, brilliance, and madness. He was to become a famous character in British military history because he managed to persuade the great Wellington that his peculiarities indicated genius as a cavalry commander. In 1809, during the Peninsular War, Wellington was to entrust Erskine with the Light Division. "A more unfortunate choice," rules the *Dictionary of National Biography*, "could not have been made. His recklessness nearly ruined the division on more than one occasion." Erskine's most famous exploit was to launch his troops after the retreating enemy in a heavy fog only to find, as the fog lifted, his division faced "with the whole *corps d'armée* of Marshall Ney." The troops were with great difficulty extracted by the brigadiers. As his symptoms of insanity increased, Erskine rose to ever higher command in the British military effort against Napoleon until his brain completely boiled over and he was cashiered from the army. In 1813, he jumped out of a high window in Portugal. He left behind testimony to Dyckman's effective labors: "a brilliant income" of between £9,000 and £10,000 per annum.

Like the elder Erskine, the younger was shy in the civilian world, but where the father had found refuge in appreciative conciliation, the younger depended on fast footwork. Face to face with the smoldering Dyckman, he continued the apologetic stance of his letter to Adam. If he spoke as he wrote, his words poured over each other half incoherently in nervous jerks. Dyckman remembered assurances "that he will cheerfully pay not only what I have suffered for his want of punctuality, but also my expenses from America and return." Dyckman urged £1,500 plus the £1,000 needed to cancel the annuity. At this, Erskine made a quicksilver turn into shrill belligerence. "After much consultation and by far too much altercation," he finally agreed to paying £2,100. Then he was all eagerness to sign an agreement at once. But Adam had elicited from Dyckman a promise that he would not "catch" the volatile baronet "by surprise." Dyckman therefore insisted that Erskine have the paper drawn up by his man of business. This would have been a serious error had Erskine been in the habit of paying attention to documents merely because he had signed them.

They agreed to close the deal at States's London lodging on October 1. As States waited triumphantly, a stranger appeared and asked brusquely *"to see my papers."* A quick look, and he announced that, according to law, the delays in payment were Dyckman's own fault: "Had I drawn regularly or properly, the money would have been regularly paid." Dyckman had no right to interest, or to reimbursement for losses or the cost of the trip to England. A thousand pounds to cancel the bond, two hundred pounds for installments not yet paid — that was all. After the man departed, States realized that in his "alarm and astonishment," he had failed to ascertain his caller's name. He had been Charles Stewart (Stuart), Erskine's man of business.

Surely the baronet would be "more liberal" as an aristocrat not impressed by "little calculations." Off to Scotland again. The baronet was plagued with callers; he could spare only a minute. He proved impressed with Stewart's "legal ideas. . . . The object seemed to be to *beat* me down as low as possible." When Dyckman argued that surely there was more to the situation than technicalities of law, Erskine said he "lamented" that he could not agree. Dyckman replied that if Erskine "listened to the erroneous calculations of Stuart, he would be sorry for it." The baronet would brook no such talk from a commoner. Becoming "so painfully affected" that "I could not speak," Dyckman fled into the Edinburgh streets.

Even in his own farmhouse, with his wife and children beside him, Dyckman had feared madness. Now he wrote Robertson from Edinburgh (and scratched it out), "My sensations have at times so overcome me that I have been stopped by people on the street, public streets, arrested by the agony of my look which I could not conceal." His worry concerning what would become of his family "renders me incapable of conversing with or seeing anyone — and obliges me to confine myself lately to my rooms."

But he did call on Sir William. He had regained control of himself. When Erskine offered to pay £1,500, Dyckman replied that if the baronet "*really*" considered this proposal "reasonable . . . the business is finished, as I have repeatedly mentioned I would leave it to him. But, knowing what I thought of the treatment received," Erskine said he would consult Adam first. He finally put in writing that, if Adam agreed, he would pay £2,000.

On the basis of "Sir William's word for the performance of his promise," Dyckman handed over the bond, executed in 1788 by Erskine's father, on which his whole claim rested. He even signed his name where asked to, although he realized it was at a place where writing could be inserted over his signature.

Confident that the Erskine matter was now for all purposes solved, Dyckman was off to Ireland to settle matters with the Bruen estate. Thinking that he might need countenance, he used his letters from American Federalists to the American ambassador to call himself to the attention of various high officials. The Bruen executor he had a letter to, Colonel King, proved too sick to see him, and Mrs. Bruen, whom he had known in the old days, was away, but the executor he could reach, Robert French, received him in the most cordial manner. After he had made his presentation, French "repeatedly assured me he was satisfied that I had a just claim to a handsome recompense. . . .

He proposed that as Mr. Adam was a much better qualified judge of the quantum to leave it to him." When Dyckman objected that he was already giving Adam too much trouble, French said he would write the letter himself. After two days, Dyckman called to pick up the letter and was told that it had been sent.

"Not doubting the truth of this, I hurried off by the first packet, and, though ill with gout, travelled night and day till I reached London. . . . In a few days, I called upon Mr. Adam and found what you will hardly credit." Adam had received no letter from French. But he had received a letter from Erskine, declining totally to "fulfill the engagement . . . to which he had pledged his honor."

To Robertson, Dyckman wrote, "So my journey of twelve or fourteen hundred miles has terminated in ruinous expenses rewarded by disappointment aggravated by being trifled with and actually deceived. Can you credit it, sir, and at the same time believe these people have their senses, knowing as they do that the stability of their fortunes depends upon the person they have so wantonly provoked and with whom they seem to sport?" Since "my humble solicitation for compassion to a faithful and meritorious servant" had been scorned, he would change to "positive demands." He would compel those whose "fortunes I have saved from ruin" to "save me from want and poverty!"

Robertson hurried off a note to Adam begging him to intercede with both Erskine and French. "Poor Dyk seems perfectly worn out with disappointments and I am afraid might be drove to such steps as might give these gentlemen more trouble than they are aware of. At the same time, Dyk would certainly involve his own character, which I think nothing but absolute despair could lead him to do."

Robertson wrote Dyckman soothingly, "Now, dear sir, as your sincere friend, allow me to act in that capacity and to advise you not to let your (but too justly provoked) resentment hurry you on to take any step that may tend to throw the smallest spot upon your fair and honorable character. It is long since the transactions you mentioned to me took place. You arranged and modified them and of course became a party concerned. The letting twenty years almost elapse without taking notice of it, would not in the opinion of liberal thinking men tend to your credit, for if you endeavor to involve one period in fresh investigations and difficulties, you must in the end involve friends and foes indiscriminately and in my opinion with little prospect of benefit to yourself — I again beg your pardon if in taking upon me the task friendship imposes, I have said a word to offend your already too much distressed feelings. . . . Enclosed I send you a draft for £100."

Dyckman replied, "No *pecuniary* consideration ever has or ever shall put to hazard my peace of mind and character, which stand as high in the estimation of those who know me as my proudest oppressors." However, he would not, "after having been tricked," accept having Sir William regard him "as an adventurer, swindler, or a sharper, instead of being received as the benefactor who saved his father and his father's reputation." He was soon to imply, by referring to himself as Sir William's "greatest benefactor," that the highborn cavalry general would without him have been little. "By no means his dependent as he is pleased to view me," Dyckman was in fact "the patron of Sir William and his family."

It had been some months since States had heard from Betsey. On his return from Ireland, he had found at long last a letter, but it brought him dreadful news of his infant daughter. "The first happy moment I have experienced for many weeks," Betsey wrote, "was the one that I received your inestimable letter of the 10th July. I got it last night. Dear welcome paper, never shall it quit my bosom while there is a bit remaining! But welcome as it was it had cost me many tears. In it you beg God to bless your dear Letty. Your prayer is heard. He has blessed her and taken her to himself. But, oh how hard a trial for her miserable mother to give her up! . . .

"When will the happy moment of your return arrive? Is it possible that only three months have passed? Bitter and long and dreary indeed have been the days and nights of your absence — — — but let us not despair. The dear departed angel is happy. Our loss is her infinite gain. We will look forward to better times.

"Mamma is much the same in every respect as when you left her. She now calls Betsey incessantly as she used to call States and when I offer to go never fails to remind me I need not hurry for I have no *baby now* to call me home. Too true indeed I have not.

"My dear Liffe, what a rich repast is your dear letters! How greedily do I devour them. Indeed, it is the only comfort that in your absence I can know, for I cannot even caress my dear Corne but the heartbreaking recollection of the one that is gone dampens all the pleasure. Oh my dear Letty! Never will I cease to mourn her loss. But why do I distress you with my troubles? Perhaps at this moment you stand as much in need of consolation as I do.

"That dreadful distance. My head turns when I think of it. Oh, that I could be sure you are well and happy! I think then I would be so too. It seems but little consolation that your letters say you are well, when I recollect how many days and weeks are past since you wrote them.

"But if I can I will change the subject for one less painful. I have been ill for some days past, but am now much better."

Betsey was doing the best she could with the farm, and was nursing an alcoholic hired man who she felt had damaged his health by giving up drinking. He was to wander away, but,

[167]

being too sick and weak to do any work, he returned to the farm. She put him in a room over the barn and nursed him until, to her tears, he died.

Death was ever in her letters: "Oh, my dear life, poor dear Ma . . . expired yesterday without a groan." States replied, "Yours, dear Betsey, has informed me that the hope I had of once more seeing my dear and respected mother, like most of our hopes in this life, was fallacious. But she is assuredly gone to receive her recompense for her long and patient sufferings from that Being she adored and served. Never was a better, kinder, tenderer parent. You say, my dear life, it must be a consolation to me that I respected her as a mother and did my duty as a son. Sometimes I have thought so too, but now she is no more I accuse myself of want of affection in leaving her amongst children selfish and unfeeling, who, quarreling with each other from principles of avarice, neglected that parent whose life was a life of care and anxiety for them. Happy indeed am I in the assurance that you, my love, left her nothing to wish in your power to do for her. Blessed be God that she died so easy and that her faith in her redeemer was never shaken. Her spirit is now with our little cherub, both perhaps anxiously watching our conduct here, hoping that when we also depart from hence we may *all meet again*. What a consoling thought, my beloved wife. It is not sufficient to counterbalance all the trivial disappointments we have and still may meet with here?"

CHAPTER FIFTEEN

Defeat in Victory

A<small>FTER</small> his reappearance in the wounding but potentially rewarding terrible large world, Dyckman had revealed no overwhelming eagerness to get back to the rural Hudson River valley, to Betsey's chaste breast and quiet mind. Despite his nervous spasms, or perhaps in part because of the vent they gave to his tensions, he was demonstrating amazing resilience. Yet he might well have cracked, even died, had he not found in London a family to take him in. It was the family of William Cobbett, one of the most powerfully pugnacious public men in all English history. Cobbett is often rated second only to Dean Swift as a murderous political satirist.

Seven years States's junior, Cobbett was a massive man, tall, broad, and somewhat overweight, blond with light eyes, whose rectangular head was so wide that despite his extensive forehead it seemed almost square. He was a handsome man, with wide-sweeping eyebrows. A strong but not ponderous nose descended with no break from his brow. His glance was keen, frank, and piercing. His expression varied between outraged determination and charming benevolence.

Born poor, Cobbett had enlisted as a common soldier in the British army. He quickly became a sergeant-major to whom his aristocratic superiors were glad to delegate responsibilities which he eagerly grasped. He saw no fighting but he saw the soldiers around him suffer from hunger. Discovering that a quarter of their rations was being deflected to the already groaning tables of the officers, he resigned from the army, returned to London, and made public charges. Then he received such a runaround as Dyckman was now receiving, and was finally warned that he would be arrested and imprisoned on trumped-up evidence of treason. He fled to France and then to the United States, where he met Dyckman.

The French revolutionaries were at war with much of Europe, including England. This polarized political opinion in the United States. The Jeffersonian Republicans regarded the French Revolution as a continuation of the American: a French victory would further "the rights of man," and French defeat would clamp aristocratic shackles on everyone, including the free citizens of the United States. But the Hamiltonian Federalists believed that the local effect of a French victory would be a "leveling" of all property and the erection of guillotines in American squares. Hearing in Philadelphia, where he had settled, mobs howling insults to the British Crown and demanding war on England in the French cause, Cobbett found himself overwhelmed with British patriotism and launched his career as a virulent pamphleteer. He smote the Jeffersonians hip and thigh, and over the head too. Driven from Philadelphia by libel suits, he moved to New York. Dyckman became "one of the most intimate friends I had in America."

In the polarization of political opinions, there had been only one direction for Dyckman to go. Although no record reveals that he held any office beyond being a delegate from his local Episcopal church to a diocesan convention, yet the Federalist leader in New York, John Jay, characterized him as a "good Federalist." After he had settled in with Cobbett, Betsey wrote him, "Two such men must be agreeable to each other. . . . The company you meet there must be very pleasant. All men of sense and your own sentiments."

Why did Cobbett, who cast himself as the scourge of venal ministries, countenance Dyckman's defense of the quartermasters and Dyckman's personal claims? Striking out as his emotions of the moment demanded, Cobbett opened himself on many fronts to charges of inconsistency. His objection to corruption was that it robbed the poor to enrich the rich. Dyckman was fighting against wealthy men for his rights, suffering injustices that reminded Cobbett of his own early difficulties. As for the whole structure of upper-class interest, that was too huge a part of the society and the times for anyone to visualize overthrowing it short of such a horrendous revolution — God forbid! — as was going on in France. Indeed, the menace of that revolution, the ominous murmurings of the British poor made it seem unwise to recognize any deeply ingrained malignancies in the British system. Like the revered establishment lawyer Adam, Cobbett, the bullhorn of acceptable radicalism, stressed, in relation to Dyckman, lack of adequate payment while raising no objections to the services for which payment was denied.

Another cause of Cobbett's support for Dyckman was compassion. Concerning Dyckman, he wrote in 1802, "I have been an eye witness of all his cares, his embarrassments, his sorrows, and his sicknesses, and if ever man suffered more than other men, during the last two years, Mr. Dyckman is that man."

Cobbett was one of the most egotistical of men. After he had taken up a cause, he regarded himself as its only effective champion — and always in the right. Being his houseguest could not have been easy — many would have found it impossible. But Dyckman had a gift for conciliation, for getting on. If sometimes hysterical, he was not himself given to laying down the law. A powerful and able bully can well use a companion who does not invite him to wrath, but yet has enough substance to keep him interested.

Cobbett lived above the bookstore he kept, "at the Crown and Mitre," in a house Dyckman described as "a palace." Not secluded in a little alley, as Mrs. Tait's had been, it was on the roaring thoroughfare of Pall Mall. The great world moved within and without. Yet Mrs. Cobbett was a warm and simple soul who, while her husband reveled in self-education, had remained illiterate. She was only two years older than Betsey. Because of her husband's widely published praises, she has gone down in history as the perfection of domestic sweetness. As his own young wife had done, she mothered Dyckman.

In January, 1801, States's gout took a most dangerous turn. The disease started in his hand but moved to his stomach and his head. He was (as he put it) "taught to consider myself" mortally ill. However, in a letter to Betsey, he played down his illness; the doctors had prevented the gout from reaching his stomach. "Much am I indebted to Mrs. Cobbett for her kind care and attention. She is an excellent woman and much respected by many very *genteel* people. She is visited by many ladies in their own carriages. It is a little awkward that you never mentioned her in many of your letters, though I believe it is my fault, not having mentioned her properly to you."

Jealousy has many faces. Betsey, who would have loved ministering to States herself, resented the other woman who nursed her husband. States had to poke at his wife several times before she finally wrote a letter to Mrs. Cobbett, which she sent to States for his approval. He handed it on, reporting that the warmhearted matron was so delighted to be thanked by States's wife that she showed the letter to all her friends.

Dyckman received in mid-April, 1801, three bonds of £1,000 each from the Bruen estate: one payable in one year, the next in two, and the last when Dalrymple's accounts were finally settled. States explained to Betsey that, as all bore interest, he hoped the bonds would not be paid off. They would then be better than an annuity. An annuity would lapse with his death, while the interest would go on, taking care of little Corne.

The Bruen estate also gave him £1,000 to reimburse his expenses. With this, so States continued to Betsey, he would "replace the books a painful necessity compelled me to part with, when my income from this country was stopped and I in vain looked around for friendship. I acknowledge it is extravagant to do so, but I must sacrifice a little to pride as well as prudence." A thousand pounds was the basic value of the Erskine annuity that had started Dyckman in the whirl that still continued.

Even before the Bruen money had come in, States had felt impelled to an extravagance deeply rooted in his family past. During the more than a century that they had been in America the Dyckmans had been orchardists. States bought a quantity of fine fruit trees — some so valuable that he feared that if they were identified they would be stolen from his fields — and his letters to Betsey were for a while as much concerned with their reception and planting as with how much he missed his wife and son. He instructed Betsey to send him some samples of the fruit. When he discovered that the little packages, instead of being kept together in the hold of the vessel that brought them, had been stuffed in this cranny and that, he became in his search for them so frantic that he was afraid a description of his feelings would too upset his Betsey. Eventually, he sent apples to Adam and others, even presuming to address a gift of twelve to the Princess of Wales. He was delighted by the polite letter of thanks from one of Her Highness's ladies-in-waiting.

States denounced to Betsey the high cost of living in England. "Clerks in the public offices, who when I was here before maintained their families decently upon 250 and 300 a year, have their salaries increased to 500 and live not near as well." He himself had been forced to pay "from two shillings to three and six for nectarines and peaches such as we would not even eat." But the rich were living so high "that you must conclude money to be worth almost nothing, for notwithstanding the war, you see nothing but dissipation. . . . This consideration obliges me to own that the bank of the Hudson is the only place for us. God grant we may possess the farm in peace!"

In writing to Betsey during January, States had tossed off that he might be able to sail home in April. This being pure moonshine, he forgot the remark, but Betsey took it seriously and, assuming he would be on the ocean, did not write.

The last letter States did receive showed little Corne as ill, and he interpreted the subsequent silence as Betsey's lack of fortitude to tell him that Corne had died. On the first of April, he wrote, "Indeed, my poor Betsey, the last fortnight has been the most wretched I ever experienced." On the 18th he told her he was "embittered by her silence." By June 28, he had decided that it must be Betsey herself who was dead. He would sail for New York were he not afraid he would miss a letter or be unable to face what he would find when he arrived. "I must await the blow which in apprehension even has almost destroyed me."

Betsey had been following the shipping news. Shortly after each vessel from London had come into New York she anticipated footsteps on the driveway. How much time she spent lingering by the gate; how much looking out the window! When instead of her husband, she received letters upbraiding her for not writing, she was furious. She was far from placated by her husband's *jeu d'esprit* that would have made her laugh in the good old days. He sent her a satire, complete with bad doggerel, he had written on a British failure to attack in Spain, adding, "My dear girl, if this, call it what you will, causes one curl of health to visit your cheek, or if it has chased one painful thought from your mind, then I am amply repaid. My intention was to make you smile." Smile indeed!

"Oh my Liffe, how distressed your last letter made me. I cannot live under your displeasure. I am sorry I left off writing at all, but it was certainly not owing to negligence. Dearest Liffe, why do you not return? I have borne your absence till now. Now it is intolerable. . . . If you do not come in June, I believe I shall be tempted to come look for you."

Particularly annoying were her husband's repeated statements that he was driven to violating what she considered his duty to her by what he asserted was his duty to her: making a lot of money to keep her and her child from humiliation and perhaps even want. "I do not write a word about business," she stated, "for you know that whatever satisfies you will amply satisfy me." She had not touched the last sum of money he had sent her: "The first was quite sufficient."

It was July 9, after almost four months of silence, that States finally received letters from Betsey. They "removed me from the lowest despondency to perfect happiness." However, he wished "that you would reconcile yourself to the *absolute necessity*," which was "infinitely more" painful to him than to her, "and must yet a little longer be endured." He was "a little surprised and disappointed that you did not express *some* satisfaction that the business with Mr. French concluded so well. You barely say that *'whatever satisfies me will be perfectly so to you.'* . . . It is for your sake I remain, for I repeat it, dear Liffe, that language is inadequate to express the impatience of my soul to fly to you."

In other letters, States confided to his Betsey another motivation. He admitted that, although he had promised Bruen's executors that he would stay till Dalrymple's affairs were settled, he could easily persuade them that he had "already done as much as possible." But he could not "as easily persuade myself to let that fellow off so lightly. . . . Oh, why do I forebear to make that wretch Sir William Erskine feel my resentment?" Erskine's friends had assured Dyckman that "his mind is not yet sound," but the American would accept no plea of insanity. It had become for the man who squandered such large sums in the service of pride, no longer a matter of money. It was a matter of proving who was the better man, of personal revenge against the aristocrat who had dared first to ignore him and then to condescend.

Because publicly disgracing Erskine would by extension damage the Bruen family that had "acted honorably," Dyckman was forced to treat the bad baronet "with a forebearance he little deserves." The furious creditor had to satisfy himself with drafting threatening letters some of which he may have dispatched. "The law, I believe, protects you from arrest [Erskine was a member of Parliament], but I trust it will not shut the eyes and ears of the world, and I will use my best endeavors that the public shall both see and hear the ungenerous treatment your greatest benefactor has met with from you."

Erskine was relying on fast footwork, as usual. He popped in and out of London. Adam managed to corner him at Alice's Coffee House and hurried off a messenger to Dyckman saying that the baronet was willing to enter into "an arbitration bond," that Dyckman should agree instantly before Erskine got away. Dyckman's agreement having been rushed back to the coffeehouse, Erskine put it in his pocket and, as he walked out, assured Adam that he would sign before he returned to Scotland.

Dyckman took to standing in the street, keeping a watch on Erskine's London mansion. There was a random coming and going of the baronet's carriage, and then footmen appeared bearing luggage. Sir William himself emerged from the door in a traveling costume. Dyckman appeared at a run. As powdered footmen looked blankly into space, Dyckman stood on the step of the carriage. He refused to budge until Sir William signed an arbitration bond that put decision in the hands of Adam, a representative of Erskine's, and, if necessary, an umpire appointed by these two.

States carried off the paper in triumph, but the baronet soon refused to have anything to do with the arbitration. He would himself appoint a single individual who would decide. As the winter of 1801–1802 came on, States wrote Betsey, "I seem to have lost sight of S.W.E., though I have by no means lost my *hold* upon him, I shall bring him to before spring."

States Dyckman and William Cobbett were among those inhabitants of England who were most strongly opposed to the forces of the French Revolution, most determined that the armies of Great Britain should thrash Napoleon, most fearful that French triumphs would detonate revolution at home. They viewed with horror and Cobbett fulminated in print against the negotiations which in 1802, through major concessions to the enemy, brought the Peace of Amiens between England and the armies on the Continent. In London, the war-weary population rejoiced; to Dyckman's expressed horror they took the horses out of the carriage of a French representative and pulled him triumphantly through the streets.

Word went out that all Londoners would illuminate their windows to celebrate the signing of the preliminary treaty. Cobbett's opposition was notorious and his house was conspicuously on that main thoroughfare, Pall Mall. He announced in his newspaper, *Porcupine and Anti-Gallian Monitor*, that he would not light up, and went to the authorities for protection. They expressed unconcern. Mrs. Cobbett was sent elsewhere; the servants seem to have fled. But Dyckman volunteered to back up with his frail physique the burly propagandist.

That night, as darkness engulfed London, Pall Mall was brightened by candles in the windows of every other house, but in front of Cobbett's house extended a patch of gloom. The gloom was soon inhabited. Dyckman had been subjected to a mob before, when the King's birthday dinner at Albany had been broken up, but that mob had been small and led by men he knew. Their intervention incited indignation more than terror. Now fear walked.

Hundreds of protestors, many of them ruffians from the nearby wharves, came running in from Pall Mall's two directions. The street congealed into a solid mass of heads with hooting mouths under upraised arms that often waved cudgels. No police appeared. From the illuminated windows across the way, faces looked on with amusement: there was no glance of sympathy. As Dyckman told the story, he and Cobbett were all alone. The pugnacious propagandist had undoubtedly armed both himself and his slight companion, yet that would avail little if the mob broke in.

The mob was at first "jovial." Shouted insults elicited mocking laughter that echoed from the sides of the street. Then stones began to fly. It was not long before every window in Cobbett's house was smashed. Mud was thrown in through the holes in the glass. By now, individual catcalls were drowned in a multitudinous roar of human rage. There was a rush to smash the main door. It was a solid door, reinforced by heavy iron bars, but it rocked, teetered, and was clearly coming down.

At this moment, Cobbett, surely to States's relief, screamed that he would illuminate. He could not make himself heard. Dyckman dashed for a candle, lit it with a trembling hand, and held it in a high and conspicuous window. Other candles appeared in Cobbett's hands. These fixed in position, the two men dashed for more, carrying them to view as fast as they could without blowing out the flames.

The crowd cheered. Hats flew into the air to be followed by little whirlpools of action as the owners sought to retrieve them. The assaults on the doors were abandoned, and the crowd returned to its holiday mood. But everyone was having too good a time to go home. Dyckman and Cobbett rushed around over the broken glass under the windows, tending the thin flames, fearful lest a diminution reactivate the rage. Hour after hour, until rising dawn washed away candlelight.

Shortly after this crisis, States moved from the Cobbetts' lodgings. He wrote Betsey that he would confide his reasons in his next letter but, although she kept asking him, he never explained. Speculation can go wildly afield. The best guess is signaled by his being on the next day, as a result of the riot, "in the utmost trouble." He may well have been ashamed to confess to Betsey that his nerves would not permit further exposure to the batterings likely to be brought on by Cobbett's unabated belligerence. No break with the Cobbetts was involved. Mrs. Cobbett continued to nurse him during recurrent attacks of gout.

William Alexander, the single arbiter Erskine had appointed, wrote Adam, "You think Dyckman entitled to a considerable. part of what he claims. I do not see at present how . . . I can make him the allowances he asks." Alexander might be able to do something towards meeting the costs of returned bills, but Dyckman's other claims, "for the sale of an estate, for the expense of borrowing, travelling expenses, etc., etc. . . . seem out of all sight." Alexander closed with a sentence pregnant for Dyckman's future: "I hope I am soon to congratulate you on being solicitor to his Royal Highness." His Royal Highness was the King's brother, the Duke of York, who was notorious for making money out of his role as commander in chief of the army.

Dyckman was indignant at Alexander's effort to apply to him the "mercantile or even strictly legal point of view" which his employers had always fought, with his help, in their dealings with the Commissioners. As a group, Dyckman's clients considered Erskine in the wrong. But when the time limit for Alexander's mediation lapsed, Erskine threatened that, if Dyckman did not agree to extend what had become so manifestly to his disadvantage, he would cut off all negotiations, repudiating forever any promise he might have made. How was the baronet to be brought to terms?

Dyckman had an idea. Sherriff had been a great admirer of the senior Erskine and would be damaged if a general scandal were raised. But he had contributed nothing during Dyckman's new stay — and he was a nervous old man. Dyckman wrote Dalrymple, "My view is to obtain such an interference or aid from General Sherriff as will procure me something like justice at least, or, in the event of his declining to interfere, that I may be considered as totally free of any blame in consequence of the unreserved communication of all the private papers I have in my possession." Dalrymple wrote Sherriff an endorsement of Dyckman's claims, as did Adam. But the determining blow was entrusted to the man in all England from whom it would be the most terrifying!

"Sir," William Cobbett wrote, "The liberty I take in addressing this letter to you, with whom I have not the honor to have the smallest acquaintance, will I trust find an apology in the poignant grief of my friend." About to depart for America, Dyckman "proposes to leave papers relative thereto in my hands, with a power to act in his stead. I have not refused him; I cannot refuse him, but I hope in God, sir, you will have both the power and the inclination to spare all the parties the trouble and vexation (to say nothing else) that a rigorous prosecution of this suit must inevitably lead to. . . .

"This letter, sir, is written to you as to a man of honor, and in full confidence that you will not communicate its contents to Mr. Dyckman, who might suppose that I took this secret method of procuring a settlement previous to his departure, lest his claim should prove unfounded, and lest I should thereby lose a part, at least, of what he owes me."

The passage about debts to Cobbett was undoubtedly included to give verisimilitude to the idea that Dyckman had not been consulted and was not in a position to stop Cobbett however much pressure the quartermasters put upon him. Dyckman kept in his files a copy of the letter.

Sherriff was frightened half to death. He gave Dyckman notes for the enlarged sum States was now demanding: £1,500 in addition to the annuity (which was not included as obviously collectable). One half of the £1,500 was to be paid in two years, the other in three, if by these dates Dyckman had not received from Erskine equivalent sums. This had the double effect of assuring payment, and putting his debts in the hands of a man it would be much less to Erskine's taste to give the runaround.

Sherriff was extremely nervous about what he had been frightened into doing. Suspecting that Erskine would resent the interference, he did not write directly to the baronet. He wrote Adam, hoping for his approval and wishing him to inform Erskine. Erskine, in the meanwhile, was finding pleasure at the thought of having maneuvered Dyckman into the alternatives of accepting unfavorable arbitration or getting nothing. When he finally learned of Sherriff's interference, he expressed rage at the busybody's efforts to foist on him debts he did not acknowledge and had no intention of paying.

In danger of having to pay the obligations himself, Sherriff wrote Erskine pleading letters: he was seventy years old and would have difficulty meeting the notes. The general was reduced to the fatuousness of asking Dyckman to intercede for him with Erskine. Eventually, Erskine assured Sherriff that, after a further delay as "punishment" for the old man's interference, he would meet the notes. The baronet never kept his promise.

Through frightening Sherriff, Dyckman had secured the money which it had originally been the mission of his trip to collect. To Mr. Corne he expressed "satisfaction" with the settlement, but added mildly that it was not "entirely to my wishes." He had, in fact, utterly failed to realize his vow "to make that wretch, Sir William Erskine, feel my resentment." The baronet, secure in his superior station, had scorned, tricked, and eluded the American. To Betsey, Dyckman wrote that he would under no circumstances move his family to England. "I like not this country, nor would you, as well as our own. Here we would be *nobody*."

CHAPTER SIXTEEN

Rich Cargo

AFTER Dalrymple, French, and Robertson had promised that each would give Dyckman an additional £1,000 if he successfully steered the accounts through final Treasury approval, Dalrymple wrote Adam, "He means to stay here this winter [1801–1802], at which I am well pleased." Betsey would obviously not be pleased. He wrote her one of his most emotional letters, reminding her that the humiliations of poverty had driven him "away from you despite feelings which at the same time tore my heart strings, and this same consideration lays affection a struggling sacrifice on the altar of duty."

He was now in a position to clear his financial slate at home. He was executing a draft that would wipe out his debt to the frightful Mrs. Douglas. He would pay Mr. Corne the £2,000 that would enable him to recover full title to his farm. "As I never saw or shall see a spot I prefer," he would return to the farm, but only if he could gain possession of the neighboring property belonging to his brother Ben. Betsey should dicker.

When the *Maryland*, on which he had most recently promised to sail, arrived at New York Betsey would have to satisfy herself with boxes on boxes of presents: for little Corne, for States Brewer, for Sill, the faithful servant Betsey had blessed as being a mother to her. Betsey's own presents — clothes, jewelry and half a bird of paradise — were so valuable that Captain Webb had agreed to smuggle them past customs. She would wear them "in health and spirits. . . .

"You will find enclosed bills for what your things cost," but the bills were only for her perusal. Now that prosperity was showering on him, he no longer felt the need to show off. Rather the opposite. "Those who cannot judge of my affection should not be permitted to judge of my conduct, (or extravagance as people might call it). Your approbation is all I wish."

The Commissioners were bored and bothered and even menaced by the investigation that had gone on so long and caused so much controversy. They could not be obviously lax, but when they had been strict, they had been turned back by the Lords of the Treasury and even an act of Parliament. Powerful men, including much of the military establishment surviving from the American War, were specifically on the quartermasters' side. And there was always the pressure for exerting tolerance and discretion towards incursions by high officials into the public purse.

States had the gift of making himself so agreeable to the Commissioners that they were inclined not to fight him too hard. His personal problems with Sir William Erskine appealed to the sympathies of men themselves eager to profit from the largesse of the great. And States was hospitable. He treated the Commissioners at dinner, at the theatre, and public gardens, took them on jaunts in the country. For those of his "*good friends*" to whom money could not be offered, he procured such valuable presents as "an expensive watch" with "the happiest effect."

When public opinion had been inflamed by the vast costs of a war that had ended in humiliating defeat, the investigations of the quartermasters had become adversary proceedings. But that was almost a generation ago. Now the need was for cooperation in forging a report that would be accepted by Dyckman's employers, not dishonorable to the Commissioners, and likely to be approved by the Lords of the Treasury. Only thus could the seemingly endless bickering be ended.

Dyckman came up with a brilliant scheme for evading the twin impeding issues: that the quartermasters had doubled as proprietors and that the Crown had been prevented from determining, in order to discover whether it was justifiable, the extent of their profits. States's suggestion was that, on the assumption that they had adequately remunerated themselves as proprietors, the quartermasters be denied what was commonly granted for carrying through meritorious services. States's clients should be allowed nothing more than they could demonstrate they had in their official capacity under due authority paid, even if to themselves. Although this compromise provided a solid base for procedure, it involved, as Dyckman pointed out, inducing the Commissioners "to unsay all they had said and undo all they had done, and even contradict their own statement to Parliament. . . . It cost me near three weeks contest with the *Inspector General* and through him the board to establish the point."

Establishing the point carried the investigation back to the procedure which had enabled Dyckman to secure approval for the accounts of the earlier quartermasters in the earlier investigations. His task was again to justify each total that appeared on the books. This "required that intimate knowledge that I alone possess. . . . It required the horses to be taken at the high rate of from twenty to twenty-five guineas, a difficult feat to maintain." Dyckman unearthed with effect the report, hitherto disbelieved, of Clinton's army board that had met in New York during 1782.

In hundreds of small ways — 133 drivers allowed in one operation instead of 121 — Dyckman upped the total. He felt he deserved the greatest rewards for his cleverest achievements, and thus he dwelt to his patrons on his most ingenious devices. While putting over £40 per wagon, because that had been passed by the New York board, he procured extra money for the buckets attached to the wagons, although they had been specifically included to justify the original estimate.

His favorite démarche remained his having collected for "horses said to have been shot for glanders." This charge had originally been "an experiment" which he had tried for Bruen's accounts in 1782, encouraged by the ease with which anything proposed was still being accepted. The quartermasters had then been credited with £7,000; twenty years of interest had doubled the sum. Now, he proposed that, if he got a similar charge through in the new accounts, the money, being altogether of his own creation, should be given him "as a small recompense" for his services. Meeting reluctance, he contended that he was getting the charge included twice, the second sum being concealed under other items in a way he could explain.

His patrons preferred less lavish payment. When in October, 1802, a report amazingly favorable to the quartermasters — only £33,000 disallowed instead of the previous £162,632 — seemed on its way to the Treasury, Dyckman secured a promise from each of the three principals of still another £1,000 each, to be paid when everything was satisfactorily settled. But his jubilation was darkened by happenings in his private affairs.

Betsey wrote: "I have frequently mentioned the disorder I had in my head which I called rheumatic but was mistaken, for Dr. Tillery says now that it proceeds from a wounded nerve and which has affected the whole nervous system. You will smile to see me write thus who till now hardly knew I have a nerve, but though now much better, I have been so ill that at least for one night I never thought to see the light of another day. I was taken (the evening after I wrote last to you) with so violent a return of the pain in my head that Dr. Tillery thought it necessary to bleed me. Nothing but the agony I was in could have made me get so far the better of the terror I have always had of this operation as to consent, but I cannot say I found any good effect from it, for the pain was incessant for five days. During that time Tillery had ordered me to take frequent small doses of laudanum. This, from both your dislike and mine to that medicine, I had neglected to take. On the evening of the fifth, he found me so ill as to think it necessary to give me above a teaspoon of that pernicious drug, supposing me in some measure used to it by obeying his former directions. The consequences was delirium succeeded by continual fainting fits for at least eight hours. Indeed I thought every moment of that time would be the last of my existence. The horror of that dreadful night cannot be described. My poor Corne was too young to feel for me and the only friend I have, the only one I love, the only one that loves me was too far away. Towards morning I grew better. By submitting to have the inside of my cheek scarified to draw the pain down I procured an intermission long enough to take a quantity of bark, a substance from which I have found the greatest benefit as I am now infinitely better than I have been for four months past and can now look forward with hope that when the dreaded hour which I lately thought so near shall in reality arrive, I shall have the supporting presence of my beloved husband to teach me fortitude.

"I believe Dear Liffee I never troubled you with two pages entirely about myself before, but with you health fled, and I cannot say that except about two or three months last summer I have ever had even a tolerable share of it since your departure. With you, I have no doubt it will return also. On the memorable 8th of February I was so ill! How dear Liffee was you? If well, I am sure you was writing to your poor girlie. Oh, how I wish I had that letter!"

Betsey had accomplished "the only step of consequence I ever undertook without your approbation." Unable, during her husband's protracted absence, to fill in a natural manner the void left by the death of Letty, she had found "a little girl," whose "relations that she lives with were very willing to give her to me." As she "suspected opposition," and did not wish States to "blame" any of their friends or relations, "I did not make a confidant." The decision to take in the little girl, she announced firmly, had been altogether her own.

States replied, "You must not be offended when I say I would rather have wished, for reasons I cannot now mention, that you had left things as they were. I must, however, repeat that in this, as in every other action of your life, I am your debtor. If the unfortunate little girl is with you, she must now of necessity remain, though I would wish it otherwise. . . . You will, I know, be hurt by the coldness of my expression. Therefore, I once more declare I cannot sufficiently thank you in this as in every other instance of the amiability of your heart."

Betsey fully understood her husband's gentle way of expressing to her his disapproval. "I see you are even more moved with displeasure than you express. . . . Yet, I flatter myself that when you see how much I love and how deserving she is, you will be reconciled to it." She had named the newcomer Catalina, after States's beloved sister.

Betsey's communications reveal the happy ending of that sister's ordeal. Caty was now so well established in the village of Harlem that she could invite Betsey for a long visit. She moved as normally as the other member of the family, to and from King's Ferry. With no indication of strain in any direction, Betsey wrote States that the sister would like the materials that would enable her to work for herself versions of the finery that her brother had sent his wife.

Betsey wrote, raising a vision of vanished games, that Caty's little son Willy "is now sitting by me and dictates to me as follows: *'Good old dog*, if you observe that Aunt Betsey's letter is worse wrote than common, the reason is that I am at her elbow chattering and disturbing her between every syllable. Dear Good Old Dog, make haste home. I long to see you.' "

Now that States was able to send her copious funds, Betsey followed his advice to abandon serious farming and to pass the winters in New York. She was somewhat extravagant, but apologized for it to her super-extravagant husband. She justified spending much time with a man (who later became a family friend) by assuring her husband that he was a good Federalist. But there can be no doubt that fear was being added to her primary emotion, loneliness. Why did her husband make promise after promise and yet not come home? States had now enlisted her grandfather on his side (the old royalist was deeply impressed by States's friendship with his hero, Cobbett) and the grandfather was writing Betsey that a man must attend to business despite the vapors of "a lovesick girl." Yet surely her husband had already made enough money to assure them "independence and a cottage" where they could be happy together.

"Wretched, indeed, I must be the moment my confidence in you is lessened." She would, she wrote, as soon doubt his love as her own — but she sent her regards to Cobbett only "if he is a *good husband.*" Why had States never explained leaving Cobbett's household and setting up his own establishment? Finally, in January, 1803, she wrote that she would join him anywhere, "even in the seraglio."

Seraglio? The only possible such implication in the papers is Wintle's comment on Dyckman's moving during October, 1802, to a flat of several rooms at 5 Pall Mall: "You can now go on any plan you like, which would not have been pleasant on Norfolk Street." Dyckman himself explained the move to his patrons by stating that his growing infirmities forced him to have a servant always at hand.

Certainly, States, for all his visions of peace at home, found exciting the gamble in which he was engaged. It was, as he stated, "a momentous concern," in the pursuit of which he exerted skill that brought power. How could he bear to rise from the gaming table while the cards were still being played, risk the inept defeat of all he had done, not see the game through to the end, and enjoy, if it were achieved, the triumph? The money he would carry home would be symbolic of that triumph.

During the night of December 3, 1802, States was on horse-back returning to London. As he pulled out to pass a slow mail coach a carriage came up from behind him. "At a furious rate" a wheel "struck me on the knee. The shock deprived me of sensation, although it did not dismount me, or I must have been crushed in the dark by the succeeding carriages. I was taken to my lodgings in a hackney coach, by some charitable people who came to my assistance."

He believed he was dying from "the spasms and convulsions the dreadful blow brought on." For several days it seemed as if his leg would have to be amputated. However, new problems were blocking the Commissioners' report. Dyckman was forced to accept what Caty's troubles had made the family nightmare: huge doses of laudanum, so that he could fight the pain and attend "the extra boards upon it." On December 24th, the Commissioners signed the report and forwarded it to the Treasury.

The inspector general assured his friend Dyckman that all was well, and Adam heard that the "termination" had been "beyond our most sanguine hopes." But Dyckman's own situation seemed desperate. "Dr. Bailie has discovered, now the inflammation is abated, that my knee . . . is horizontally split through." It would be a long time before he could hope to stand on his leg again, and his gout had joined in.

Dalrymple made things even worse by "almost living" at States's rooms in a perpetual flap: had the Commissioners' report been strongly enough worded; how could they get a copy of the report so that pressure could be put on the Treasury? "His *disappointments*," Dalrymple explained in justification of his behavior, "have exhausted all his patience." Dyckman finally had his servant tell the general that he was too sick to see him, which induced Dalrymple to complain to Adam.

"From the justice of the claim," Dyckman wrote, "and the clearness with which it is stated, we might reasonably hope for a happy and immediate conclusion and that I should be at liberty to return to my family." Yet he feared that the business might stay at the Treasury "for months and even years, as it has done," unless "constant and incessant application compel, if I may so express myself, their Lordships' attention to it." A member of Parliament could best execute the task, but neither Dalrymple nor Robertson now had the necessary connection, "nor does anyone in the House occur to me as likely to take that trouble." But the Bruens, once the least influential of the quartermaster families, had in their prosperity gained considerable leverage on the Irish vote. They should put pressure directly on the minister, "who will, after the election, have a powerful host to contend with in the lower house."

Pressure was effectively exerted — undoubtedly Adam had a hand in it — until it seemed feasible to abandon the compromise proposal that, since the quartermasters had profited as proprietors, they should be allowed no more than the official expenses they could substantiate. Now it was suggested that what the Commissioners had ruled returnable to the Crown as unsubstantiated be granted Dalrymple as a reward for efficient service. In a brilliant tactical stroke, it was recommended that this issue be submitted to a single arbiter: the commander in chief of the army, the King's brother, the Duke of York. Never was an expedient more comprehensive and watertight.

Like everyone else, the Lords of the Treasury wanted to get the quarter-of-a-century-old investigation unstuck from their fingers without being untrue to their trust or persecuting their peers. What better auspices than a royal commander in chief! His decision was certain to favor leniency. The duke was "known to be an easy-going man"; his mistress used his influence to sell high offices in the army. Furthermore, Adam was his solicitor and friend. It was only a matter of Adam finding a suitable occasion to speak to the duke. And the duke's decision, although it involved no examination of the record and was only on one final point, would in effect countenance the entire award to the quartermasters.

On April 27, 1803, His Royal Highness declared his "decided opinion" that "no military officer should serve as a contractor, but this practice having been admitted in the American War . . . and sanctioned also by the government," should be, in Dalrymple's case, allowed. Since Dalrymple had served faithfully and efficiently the "*quantum meruit*" should be granted.

To carry out this ruling, adjustments had to be made by the Commissioners and then approved by the Treasury — this might take months — but triumph now seemed sure. The result for Dyckman's world was turbulence. His clients, no longer tied together by common danger, revived old squabbles as to who had paid what to whom, and whether it was enough. Various of the quartermasters tried to enlist States's help in demonstrating delinquencies of others. And States felt great anxiety as to how he himself would be treated when considered no longer necessary. He was swept into "a nervous fever . . . which once more threatens me with ending my days here. My physician has now so far bolstered me with *Laudanum* [he underlined and capitalized the dreaded word] that I am able to resume my pen."

Dyckman had two desires that pulled against each other. He wished in the new relationships with his clients which were now developing to be recognized as a friend and equal; and he wished his total victory to be rewarded with what he considered a suitable addition to the recompense. Had he prepared for departure to America passively the quartermasters would surely have been warm, even affectionate, in their farewells. But as he pulled at their coattails with new demands, they feared, all the more because he had so great a claim on their gratitude, that they would never get rid of him. And he did not make things any easier by exhibiting the same over-sensitivity that had made him, when hard up in America, study his neighbors for behavior at which he could take offense. Thus, when French sent him a purely business letter, he diagnosed in it "a coldness" differing "extremely from what your expressions were when I last saw you."

However imaginary were his grievances elsewhere, Dyckman had every reason to be offended with Dalrymple. The obese general, who had dithered by the sick man's bedside days on end when things were still to be decided, now wrote Adam, "Dyckman called at my door this morning. I did not receive him. I am told he thinks he is in a dying condition and longs for America.

"He has also made an unfortunate connection with some mercantile person here. The last time I saw him, he had just been arrested, the person he was connected with having been guilty of some improper conduct in the payment of sums entrusted to him. . . . I see many reasons for ending the business between us, and I trust to your friendship for doing so immediately."

Since in his extravagance Dyckman had a way of anticipating the payments due him from his patrons (and since they sometimes delayed meeting the obligations), it is quite possible that he was arrested for debt, a routine procedure for bill collectors which rarely resulted in a man with assets going to prison. (There is no evidence that Dyckman did.) No hint of any dishonest mercantile connection can be found in the existing Dyckman Papers.

During March, Adam endorsed Dyckman's services: "I think it but justice to say that his minute knowledge . . . and the opportunity he had of stating that proper view of the accounts brought it to the point where it is now." But Dalrymple persuaded Adam that States was making unfair claims.

On June 17, Dyckman wrote Adam, "It is the great value I

have ever set upon the friendship and good opinion you once honored me with which makes me feel so sensibly the coldness you now show me and of which I have not even the right to complain, for I can only repeat to you, without fear of either flattery or impertinence attributed to me, what I told General Dalrymple: that you are the only person in the world who had conferred favors on me without receiving more than the equivalent."

On June 29, Dalrymple wrote Adam, "I found Dyckman at home. He did not, on my entering, seem at his ease. Our conversation was very short. . . . I am persuaded that he had no idea of my knowing anything of his conduct with Mr. Kingston."

Dyckman's "conduct with Mr. Kingston" became the focus of suspicions. A representative of the Bruen estate, Kingston brought the matter to a head by accusing Dyckman, during a meeting in Adam's chambers, of stating that he would delay the final settlement of the accounts till a previous settlement with him had been made by all concerned. Dyckman responded angrily, "Knowing the anxiety I have experienced for the fate of the accounts, the labor I have devoted to them, the sacrifices I have made of domestic happiness to bring them from a state of ruin to a conclusion far exceeding our most sanguine hopes, I could not patiently bear such an imputation. . . . Had I met the same injurious treatment last September, when I was prevailed on to stay, those interested in the accounts would have been £128,000 poorer." However, he did not altogether deny the threat.

Adam was not amused. Perhaps he had heard that Dyckman was, in urging his claims, asserting that Adam could not judge the extent of his contribution because the pillar of rectitude had been kept ignorant of how much more Dyckman had procured for the quartermasters than they had a right to. Dyckman was soon to write Robertson that Adam would no longer communicate with him.

Yet facts were facts: Dyckman might be able, through his influence with the Commissioners, to delay or even destroy the happy ending. The three principals agreed to give him further large sums — the best evidence indicates £4,000 apiece — to be paid when the settlement was final. Dyckman had to wait in England for that moment. He remained on bad terms only with Dalrymple and Adam. During two trips to Ireland (which reveal that he was not fully crippled by his split knee), Dyckman charmed French into giving him an additional thousand pounds as a "remembrance." Robertson, the ever compliant, did not follow his cousin Adam into outrage with Dyckman.

On September 12, 1803, Dyckman was able to write, "The Inspector General showed me the account allowed and declared by the Treasury, and as this was the finis, we yesterday interred the old account into the sepulchral vault of Somerset House, after which all the clerks dined with me, and we sang a requiem over the *departed*. Amen!"

The tide which States had started flowing in Dalrymple's direction had flowed on until *mirabile dictu* it had been decided that instead of Dalrymple owing money to the Crown the Crown owed him £1,387. In total, Dalrymple had been allowed £320,729. According to the rough estimate adopted here, one hundred to one, this would be in modern currency more than thirty-two million dollars.

Despite the fact that he was an expert accountant (or perhaps because of it) the reports on his earnings Dyckman volunteered to various correspondents for various purposes are far from consistent or complete. We have only fleeting indications concerning payments of £100 or so given him informally when he was short of cash or to reimburse expenses. But there is enough evidence to conclude safely that he received in bulk from Dalrymple £8,000, from Robertson £8,000, and from the Bruen estate £10,000. His major compensation for clearing accounts totaling £320,729 equaled some £26,000. This comes to about 8.1 percent, which would be a very modest fee for a modern agent, and startlingly small for a modern lawyer.

To estimate Dyckman's total takings during his three years and nine months in England we must add the £1,500 he procured through Sherriff as an indemnity from Erskine. Legally required payments on the uncanceled Erskine annuity — overdue or then due — of £200 a year must have amounted to about £1,000. All in all, Dyckman collected at least £28,500, the rough equivalent in modern currency of $2,850,000.

Dyckman could only walk with difficulty. But as he rode in a hired coach through the London streets, his constitution sapped by ever more frequent attacks of gout, one of his legs crippled by an errant carriage wheel, he could jubilate that he was at last free to bring, as he described it, "the ship rich with cargo into port."

Had Dyckman, as he amassed his "rich cargo," been true to his claim put forward as he sailed from New York, of "integrity and uprightness"? For a man so utterly unconcerned with abstract considerations, the answer to this question, if it is to be couched in his own mental terms, must turn on the mores and morals of his time and place. Like a fish in a flowing river, Dyckman judged his movements in relation not to distant, immobile shores, but to the currents that actively enveloped him.

The battle of the quartermasters was a conspicuous, if small, engagement in a conflict far above the possibilities of such a man as Dyckman to command or in its essence comprehend. He had followed, as the experiences of his childhood had taught him to do, "the way of the world."

The campaign had for a full quarter of a century been conducted under the eyes of those who mattered; and it had been won with the sanction of a Royal Duke, the Lords of the Treasury, the Commissioners officially entrusted with guarding the Crown finances, Parliament, noblemen, high military officers. Ever since the publication of the *Seventh Report*, it had been common knowledge that the quartermasters had also been the proprietors. And, while frustrating the efforts of the Crown to determine the extent of their profits, the quartermasters had demonstrated by their extravagance that the profits had been huge. The situation was thus clear. How to react rested on a high plane of governmental policy and practice.

For years the authorities waffled, unable to make up their minds to what extent they should protect the public funds and to what extent the freedom of officeholders to achieve profits, even if immense. Dyckman had been able to supply enough seeming justification for the quartermasters' actions to make plausible a decision on the aristocratic side. This he was glad to do.

Dyckman could not have known that the idol of the Federalists, Alexander Hamilton, had said (or so Jefferson angrily contended) that the British government was a model for the world, and that corruption was an essential part. Yet as Dyckman, from his own lookout, surveyed the activity around him, he could not doubt that official perquisites fueled the system. Concerning the system itself, he felt no qualms: he admired the rich, the important, the well-born, the fashionable. What rankled was that he was so scornfully excluded as inferior by associates whose position he had buoyed up and who he learned from prolonged personal contact were no better than he.

Although the road he had traveled was so different, the former Loyalist was now occupying what had been the official position of the American Revolutionaries at the start of the Rebellion. Before independence had become an active issue, the American leaders had asked no more than the equal rights that would enable them to govern themselves. A protest written by Dyckman to Erskine (he referred to himself in the third person) could have been a paraphrase of one of the remonstrances dispatched to the British government by the First Continental Congress: "Why should he entreat from compassion what he feels himself entitled to from justice? He is weary with soliciting and imploring. There is a point beyond which even the weakest person can no longer endure oppression."

For Dyckman's negotiations with the Commissioners there were, in American experience, almost no precedents. Where bureaucracy and taxation and governmental expenditures had always been minimal, government investigations of personal finances hardly existed. But payments of tax money that required the subsequent approval of auditors had long been standard British practice. Dyckman found established procedures which he was quick to learn.

That the quartermasters' accounts were stated over and over, and that Dyckman's inspired restatements finally broke the log jam, indicated universal agreement that there was more involved than synthesizing authentic figures. There was clearly a wide area for reinterpretation, argument, judgment, conciliation. When such opportunities exist, it is natural for opposite advocates to try to overreach each other. Dyckman boasted of pulling the wool over the Commissioners' eyes, and his patrons agreed that the greater his success in this, the greater should be his remuneration. Even the righteous Adam, although kept in ignorance of some particulars, could not have doubted that to a considerable extent his clients' interests were being thus imaginatively served.

What about the bribes that were offered and accepted: entertainments, expensive presents, cash? Dyckman routinely reported such expenses to his clients, who as routinely forwarded the money.

The crux was that it was not persons but the government that was being taken advantage of. The government itself recognized the distinction in that criminal proceedings were not involved. The only potential penalty was that the recipient of public money be forced to return to the Crown what had been unsuitably collected. Most significantly, no interest was charged on sums often tremendous and held for many years.

Dyckman's relations with his clients followed a different moral code from his personal dealings whether in England or America. If in the service of the quartermasters he dissembled and took advantage, why should he not dissemble and take advantage of them? This attitude his clients accepted as part of the game.

Even in their correspondence about Dyckman among themselves, none of his associates denounced as blackmail his threats of public exposure, nor, indeed, did they express moral indignation. That he had the papers and could, if he wished, use them to everyone's damage was accepted as an aspect of the situation that, like other aspects, had to be reckoned with. It was taken as a matter of course that Dyckman might be tempted to violence by Erskine's behavior, that was acknowledged by all the others to be perfidious. However, it was assumed that, if only to protect his own reputation, Dyckman would not carry out his threats — that is unless the provocation became stronger than his associates intended to permit it to become. It was only when total victory was in sight, when all were congratulating themselves and breathing easy, that Dyckman's final threat — to sabotage the victory — excited rage and indignation. And even then only Adam and Dalrymple remained outraged. French and Robertson soon behaved as if nothing unusual had happened.

Dyckman's clients naturally felt that their payments justified their demanding that the evidence with which Dyckman had threatened them be now destroyed. Dyckman assured French that, with the exception of some documents he had entrusted to Dalrymple, "every paper which was in my possession, such as memoranda, remarks, correspondence, etc. . . . are, upon my honor, burned and destroyed." Yet he had packed for transport to America revealing documents by the hundreds.

What motives were so compelling that they induced a man who took his honor so seriously, so flagrantly to break his word of honor? Now that everything was settled, the incriminating papers only had nuisance value: it is hardly credible that Dyckman was preserving them on the chance that he might someday use them again as weapons. Much more probably, his behavior was dictated by the same personal sense of uniqueness, of hidden importance, that had made him, from young manhood, preserve his other papers through all the travels and vicissitudes of a far from tranquil career. He did not wish to change the world, but he wished to keep his own personality afloat. He intended to raise on the banks of his ancestral Hudson a mansion that would proclaim his taste and importance to the eyes of all who passed, and to posterity. How could he wipe from the record the most significant, the most exciting, the most rewarding of his adventures? Indeed, had he not broken his word of honor, this biography of States Dyckman could never have been written.

CHAPTER SEVENTEEN

Into the Dust

AFTER it had become almost certain that a satisfactory settle-ment would bring Dyckman the funds that he had been for that contingency promised, he launched on a spending spree that dwarfed all which had gone before. Although more highly priced, his purchases were what they had always been: objects of accepted luxury reflecting the conventional taste of the upper classes. As before, he resolved, probably because the veneers might peel off during the slow ocean crossing, to take no furni-ture with him, but there was much else to buy. One of the timepieces he secured was a "very small, oval watch, duplex scarpment, jewelled diamond balance, two gold enamel dials, put in a gold enamel box with four joints set with brilliants, etc.": the price was £63. As part of a purchase that came to £114 he bought "a rich dessert service painted with landscapes to order with gilded key and leaf of solid gold." Diners could, as they cleared their plates, admire the "View on the Thames," or "Cottage at Blaize Castle," etcetera. For Wedgwood, the prices were more modest: thirty-two pieces, "deep blue and white jasper cameo, subjects in compartments," cost only £13.10.18.

As always, Dyckman spent money in acts of benevolence. Cornwallis Connell wrote him, "Finding you are on the eve of leaving this country, permit me to offer you my most grateful and heartfelt thanks for your kindness to my children in general, and particularly to Margaret. It is not necessary for me to point out to you the benefits she may hereafter experience from education, which through my misfortune she must be deprived, were it not for your kind and benevolent interference."

Dyckman restored the good resolves he had expressed before his previous journey to retirement. He was, he wrote Mr. Corne, leaving £12,000 with his English bankers, which sum "I intend by the blessings of heaven shall remain untouched except the interest until the day of my death."

To Betsey, he announced on October 4, 1804, "Within three days, I shall climb the pitchy side of the *Tippo Sahib* at Devon. . . . And now, my beloved, having accomplished everything, I shall return to you in better spirits at least, if not in better health, than I left you. Care shall no more cloud my brow, though pain perhaps may. . . . Now, my dear one, all being finished, and the gout having put a final stop to my labors and exertions, economy must not only be the order of the day, but of the rest of our lives. We have now acquired, and by the blessings of heaven we will endeavor to keep it, sufficient for all our real wants, and ideal ones we will not create. This you will say agrees but ill with the invoices [for what he was sending home]. Be it so then, and call it if you please, the last sacrifice to folly. But, as I do not like the word, and can find no other that will express my meaning, we shall say no more about it. The wish of gratifying you, I will own, has perhaps carried me too far. Perhaps I have mistaken the method. Prudence might have been more pleasing to you? Then, ever dear one, I will promise that ever hereafter prudence will be my guide."

He was sailing to Charleston because by "a southern voyage" he hoped to elude his gout which normally struck with cold weather. It might, he acknowledged, help his physical condition to resettle with his family in Charleston, but his farm on his childhood river was "the only place I look forward to for peace and rest." Only if he were too sick to move when he reached

South Carolina should Betsey join him there. "Should I have the use of limbs, then I shall not want wings to fly to you in eight days. . . .

"When it shall please heaven I see you, I will boldly bid defiance to the gout and every other worldly care, for with you and dear Corne in my arms, I shall have little to fear and almost as little to wish."

Needing to protect feelings so often lacerated, Betsey could not let herself believe firmly that her husband would actually climb "the pitchy side of the *Tippo Sahib*." Yet his assurances had a new tone. His business, he admitted, was over, his coffers as full as he could make them. He no longer insisted that, between attacks of gout, he had never felt better. He foresaw that gout would "put a stop to my labors and exertions."

Distressing surely, but this admission of invalidism was also reassuring for a wife who wished her husband to come and stay home. In one of his light moments, he had written from England:

> *Again a little while and then*
> *Dear Liffee I will burn my pen,*
> *Abjure for ever prose and rhyme.*
> *The vessels pitchy side will climb*
> *Sleep five long weeks, awake to joy*
> *Clasp in my arms my wife, my boy,*
> *Swear ne'er to rove from you again*
> *But live your* slave, *your arms my* chain.
> *Now I know you smile and say*
> *That verse would run as well this way*
> *"And never more will rove about*
> *But stay at home, chained by the gout."*

States's gout had been an intimate part of the life he had shared with a woman for whom nursing the sick and weak was a passion. From England, after visiting an ailing husband with a younger wife, States had commented to Betsey that she and the wife were alike in being sentenced to nurse gouty old men — and in having husbands able to appreciate it. When little Corne carried a crutch around as a souvenir of his father, Betsey was moved to affectionate and wistful tears. However, she may well have been horrified when the long-anticipated knock sounded on her door. Standing on her threshold was a dying man.

Dyckman, it is true, was to live for more than two years, yet as Betsey was to explain, he suffered from such "constant ill-health since he returned to America," that she was never able to question him on such basic matters as whether he had drawn up a will. In London, he had been kept in motion by the momentum of obsession. Again and again, he had risen from what he feared was his deathbed, fueled by the drug his family most feared: laudanum. But, "in peace and tranquility beyond the reach of poverty" he was no longer driven. Enabled (as he had envisioned) to put his head on his wife's bosom "tranquilized" by his return, he soon collapsed.

The ends for which States had adventured to England had been completely achieved.. The humiliating poverty from which he had fled, with its implications of incompetence and vainglory on his part, had been most dramatically dispelled. And the old fights were done with. His neighbors, whom he had suspected of shunning him, now bowed to him with conspicuous respect. His wife's relatives, who had so woundingly accused him of having married their young beauty through fraud, now fawned upon him. Feeble and rheumatic now, Mr. Corne still saw him illuminated by the halo of friendship with the great champion Cobbett. And the sweet scent of his wealth made the malign, "purse-proud" Mrs. Douglas smile upon him. With his own brothers, whom he had disowned in rage, he was now again on the old close terms. He had the satisfaction of rescuing from jail in

Virginia his brother John, who had been sick and was threatened with debtors' prison. John wrote that he could only repay States "with tears of thanks." The returned traveler was happily in a position to regard this payment as more than enough.

Far off in England, such evasions and delays as had so enraged him went on. Erskine sought arcane deductions from the installments he was legally forced to pay States, and the baronet broke his promises to reimburse Sherriff who soon died, throwing his obligation to Dyckman into his estate. But eventually, one way or another, his bankers managed to collect, and, in any case, States could comfortably wait for belated payments to appear. The old rage was behind him.

As his bankers handled his business, he had no further personal contacts with the patrons who had occupied the center of his life. The bankers even took over his relationship with the Cobbetts. On his arrival in America, States had, it is true, handled a lawsuit in Philadelphia for his old friend, and sent him £500. But it was his bankers who informed him during 1803 that Cobbett, now in financial straits, felt that the American he had taken in and helped to become wealthy had not adequately rewarded him for his "time and trouble." States responded with 101 guineas which, the bankers reported, put Cobbett in a "good humor." The bankers added, "Mrs. Cobbett is a very good woman and extremely friendly and attentive to you at all times. We are not sure she is fully compensated. This you may consider of." It is hard to believe that Dyckman, the ever generous, was deaf to this appeal, but there was no restoration of personal contact with the Cobbetts.

From the Hudson Valley, Dyckman informed various correspondents that he was busy farming, but his bills reveal the opposite: few payments for seed or tools, many charges for vegetables and grain. There is no evidence of the jaunts he had loved, but only of trips to New York City, often undertaken despite illness, to straighten out his financial affairs. As Napoleon's renewed rampages were having a devastating effect on business in London, Dyckman gradually put most of his assets in American bonds.

Since he had imported no furniture worthy of his prosperity, he surely bought from the best cabinetmakers in New York, but he did not keep, as he had in London, his bills. He made no effort to catalogue his imported silver, china, glass, etc., but he did attempt a book catalogue. His library was in size — 1,314 volumes — truly impressive for its time and place: Jefferson's some 6,000 volumes, not five times as many, sufficed to get the Library of Congress started again after the city of Washington had been burned during the War of 1812. But Dyckman's catalogue reveals no systematic collecting and his efforts, during his last years, to assign his books to categories resulted in confusion: many overlappings, a fourth of his collection dumped at random into "Miscellaneous." His taste, with a suitable bow to "divinity and ecclesiastical history," ran to history and biography, poetry, "novels and romances" and particularly the theatre. Surprising is the lack, despite his friendship with Cobbett, of the political polemics so common in the eighteenth century, and also of works supporting his taste in fine furnishings. He possessed as his only one book on a subject now to him of great interest: *Walton's Cottage Architecture*.

Lacking any urge to educate his neighbors, Dyckman did not, in his plan for a new mansion house, locate his library where it would be accessible. He inserted the potentially very useful collection among the bedrooms on the second floor.

Betsey was of full childbearing age and States only in his late forties, yet the passionately maternal wife bore no more children. The "little girl" whom she had taken in to his disapproval during his absence disappears from the record. Although presumably the husband's illegitimate child, States Brewer was Betsey's, not his, protégé. When she had remonstrated that the presents sent from London failed to include any for young States, Dyckman had answered testily that she should tell young States that he loved the boy more than the boy loved him. Although presents were subsequently sent, after the father's return, Brewer also disappears from the record.

On little Corne, States doted. When the boy was ill, the father was frantic. Betsey had given as a compelling reason why her husband should return from England that she was unable to control their son. Now Corne, who was sent away to school in the village of Harlem, did badly there. A friend tried to reassure the father: "I sincerely think that though his improvement at present is very gradual, application will come with riper years, and that his attainments will not be the less for being late."*

The Dyckmans prided themselves on their hospitality, which was mentioned on both their gravestones. One Benjamin West, who seems to have been a traveler from England, wrote States after he had moved on to Philadelphia, "The manner of doing a thing is certainly not of such trivial importance as is very much imagined here. . . . It either enhances or detracts from a favor." This thought led him "to draw a contrast between the truly friendly attention I experienced at King's Ferry, and the formal reception of many on whom I have a better claim." The difference West attributed to "good breeding."

Betsey, ever the shielder of lame ducks, continued to bring them into the household. A group of her friends remembered her as "cheerful, benevolent, hospitable. Her bounty was without ostentation, her hospitality flowing from native kindness of heart."

Dyckman's major objective on his return home, beyond surcease in the bosom of his family from labor and strain and pain,

---

*Corne, always sickly, married and had a daughter, but left no other mark on the world. He died at twenty-seven.

had been to carry into reality the dream he had nurtured, during his previous stay on the Hudson, when he had been most pushed to the wall and had felt most humiliated. Then he had found what comfort he could in walking his property on Montross Point to determine the best site for a mansion house which he would build after he had triumphed over his troubles: an impressive edifice that would express for all to see his taste, and would confound his relations and neighbors who were sneering and slighting him as a pretentious pauper.

In England, he had procured the necessary money and decided on the name for his future mansion house. He had included in a business trip to the Bruen heirs in Ireland a pilgrimage through Shropshire to a once obscure hunting lodge named Boscobel, which had been for more than a century for British royalists a shrine. Deeply moved, he decided to call his dreamhouse in America Boscobel.

The historic Boscobel had been involved with the death and life of kings. In 1650, hardly more than a year after his father, Charles I, had been executed by the Roundheads, the son who was to be crowned Charles II sailed from exile in France to Scotland.

Assured that the people would rise to his royal banner, he marched into England intending to defeat Cromwell and achieve the "Restoration" that was to be accomplished almost a decade later. But at the Battle of Worcester, his feeble force was pulverized by Cromwell's powerful army. No center of power was left for the King to flee to. He was loose in the countryside while one of the greatest manhunts in history was undertaken to find him and further stamp out the royal line with a second regicide. His very presence was like a carrier of a mortal contagion: anyone who gave him food or shelter or did not report him to the authorities would, if discovered, be executed.

Protected, it was later claimed, by "miraculous providences," the King wandered for forty-one days disguised as a peasant: "A leather doublet, a pair of green breeches and jump coat (as the country calls it) of the same green, a pair of stockings with the tops cut off because embroidered . . . a pair of old shoes cut and slashed to give ease to his feet, an old greasy hat without lining, a noggen shirt of the coarsest linen, a face and hands made of reechy complexion by the help of walnut leaves." Since it seemed essential that he keep moving, his feet were torn and bleeding. Since the humbler his stopping places the safer he was, he slept in the meanest sheds and ate the roughest peasant food — it would have raised suspicion to buy even something as ordinary as a joint of mutton.

Eventually, His Majesty was told of the hunting lodge deep in the woods that was unlikely to be searched because it was inhabited only by servants. At Boscobel, Charles found a solid roof over his head, stored provisions to eat, and even a little walled garden where he could relax in the sun. At nighttime, he retired into one of two "priests' holes," tiny rooms accessible down ladders leading from disguised trapdoors. During one night of particular dangers, Charles II perched high in the branches of a huge oak tree, using as a pillow a colonel. When the colonel's arm on which the royal head rested became numb, he was driven, lest they both be catapulted to the hostilely patrolled ground, to an act he considered almost sacrilegious. He pinched the royal flesh.

"The Royal Oak" became, after the Restoration, such a mine of souvenirs that it was hacked to pieces and was replaced, according to correct dynastic descent, by a tree of similar magic because raised from an acorn of the old. Dyckman wrote Mr. Corne that he had had "the good fortune to procure a small piece," which he had had fashioned into two snuffboxes, one for Corne and another for a gentleman whose "opinions on this subject" also corresponded with his own.

In naming his intended mansion house Boscobel, Dyckman was doing more than express the royalism of those extreme Fed-

eralists who, in their terror of French revolutionary ideas, feared
that the United States would sink into ensanguined chaos if it
did not bow to the only proven system of government: monar-
chy. Far from looking up at the King as immeasurably above
him, the simply born American identified himself, in a manner
that might well horrify British aristocrats, with Charles II. He
recast a royal adventure in his own personal terms. Boscobel
would be for him, as it had been for the King, a blessed haven
from persecution and strain, from a hostile world. When stricken
in London with sickness he feared would be mortal, Dyckman
expressed to Cobbett his hope that he might live to reach "the
land of plenty, Boscobel."

Dyckman's present intentions, like his previous dreams, involved building on Montross Point: the southern end of an arc of
tableland that extended a little distance into the river. (King's
Grange had occupied the northern extremity.) States had only to
walk out of his farmhouse door, gout permitting, to decide finally the exact location of Boscobel. He chose a flat area, close to
where the ground fell not steeply to the Hudson shore. He intended to embellish the gradual decline with small, decorative
buildings, curving terraces, winding paths. A humpbacked hill
rose in the center of his view. It divided the distant outlook into
two vistas: Peekskill Bay to the north, and to the south the
widening of the Hudson into the Tappan Zee. The far shore
rose undramatically, dotted with open fields and houses. All in
all, such a location as suited his taste: not "grand and sublime"
but capable of being embellished into what the eighteenth century considered "the beautiful."

Boscobel, which still stands,* is for architectural historians an

---

* Boscobel stood at its original location on Montross Point until 1955, when the United
States Veterans' Administration, which had acquired the land for a hospital, sold the
now rundown structure to a wrecker for thirty-five dollars. Outraged neighbors are said
to have lain down before the bulldozers. The wrecker was frustrated, but no site was immediately available to which the house could be moved. Boscobel was taken apart and
preserved in pieces. It was reerected soon thereafter overlooking the Hudson in Garrison,
New York, fifteen miles north of the original location.

enigma. To begin with there is the question of who designed it? Surely not Dyckman, who had, in all his jottings and travels and book collecting, shown an unconcern with architecture. It would seem natural for him to have brought plans back with him from England, but efforts to find close prototypes there have failed, while investigations in other Hudson River mansions reveal echoes and similarities even if no actual models. On the back of a grocery bill, dated November 2, 1804, is a complete rendition for the house, more conventionally in the reigning Hudson River manner than what was eventually erected.

Professional architects grew only very sparsely in early nineteenth-century America. Houses were commonly designed by master builders under the more or less interfering eye of the owner. Dyckman's master builder was his kinsman, William Vermillye.

On both sides of the ocean, gentlemen or craftsmen almost always selected interior or exterior features from the ubiquitous builders' manuals published for that purpose in England. Research has not yet revealed any such copying at Boscobel.

The interior plan of Boscobel resembles that of similar mansion houses in emphasizing not private but public living. Guests were welcomed into a front hall which was the largest space in the house. At the far end an elaborate stairway, breaking as it rises in two wings to the bedroom floor, is visible but ritualistically separated from the public space by a skeleton partition of arches and columns. Doors open from the main hall into a large dining room on the left and on the right one drawing room behind another. Throughout the decoration is lavish and somewhat naïvely executed in the accepted manner, descended from

---

Boscobel is now maintained as a public museum. The house has been surrounded with lawns, gardens, and an orchard, reflecting States's agricultural interests. Its rooms contain furniture purchased by States and Elizabeth Dyckman, supplemented by fine examples of New York Federal furniture. All this has been made possible by the generosity of Mrs. DeWitt Wallace who, with her husband, founded *The Reader's Digest*.

the designs of the Adam brothers, with two of whose nephews Dyckman had in England been so entangled.

The facade of Boscobel is correctly in the neoclassical manner descended from the sixteenth-century Italian architect Palladio, yet the whole is dominated by an architectural invention, which if naïve, is extremely effective and, as far as is known, unique.

The second-floor central porches in Palladian structures were often fitted with awnings that could be let down to create shade. When drawn up the awning could be tied to the tops of the porches in swags. The builders of Boscobel decided to carve the swags in wood. The decision once made, semi-abstract design took over. The wooden swags hang straight up and down, the folds too shallow and regular for bunched cloth. On the pediment above the swags, the builders echoed the carved folds, enclosing them in non-representational wing-like shapes.

The line of swags is removed from its functional source by a rearrangement of the facade's central block. The crowning pediment is raised to let the swags expand laterally beyond both sides of the porch and over the supporting columns. Seconded by the presence of the columns, the swags appear to constitute an important element in holding the whole structure together and upright.

Although small in area compared with the rest of the front, the swags catch the eye as the most conspicuous aspect of the otherwise conventional facade. They bring to the sober, neoclassical elegance of the Palladian forms a holiday note, frivolous but equally elegant. It is their presence which make Boscobel stand out among its peers up and down the valley.

Boscobel was erected for the most part under Betsey's supervision, since her husband died before the house was more than a foundation and a stockpile of materials. Yet there can be no doubt that the design was in its major elements settled while States Dyckman lived. How did the man whose taste had always been so conventional become enamored of the delightful but eccentric wooden swags? It can only be said that the facade as it now stands well expressed his character: somewhat provincial for all of his worldly experience, serious, with warmth and charm.

On August 11, 1806, at the age of fifty-one, States Dyckman died. He was buried in the family plot at Kingsbridge, at the top of Manhattan Island. The mourners consumed three gallons of sherry, one of brandy, along with "tobacco pipes and cigars," in all worth £2.13.6.

A search in the deceased's papers for a will unearthed not a will but a letter that terrified. Peter Corne, who had not been well enough to go to his granddaughter or even attend the funeral, reacted, when informed, with dismay. He urged Betsey to hurry to him in New York City "as soon as propriety can permit. . . . I think it would be very imprudent as well as impolitic to bring any female companion in your train of whatever description. . . . Be careful to bring all your papers with you. Do not suffer a lisp of what you know of their contents to escape you." On second thoughts, Corne added a P.S.: "Read the contents then burn the letter for fear of inquisition."

Betsey replied that she was "far from being fit to comply with your kind request of coming to you. . . . Perhaps in a month or two I will be able to make you a visit."

There is no record that the frightening letter presaged any trouble. We know nothing of its purport beyond the fact that it in no way mitigated Betsey's grief for her husband. Although his death had been foreseeable from the moment of his return from England, the actual loss utterly prostrated the wife who had nursed him so passionately. Nine months passed before she could find the fortitude to ask Douglas & Shaw in London whether her husband had left with them a will. She would have written sooner "had I been able. Even now I find myself quite unequal to the attempt."

For Dyckman's gravestone, Betsey wrote: "His manners were

polite, his taste refined, his conjugal love was pure, his parental strong, his hospitality sprung from benevolence, his charity from feeling and sense of duty. Highly esteemed in life, he was sincerely lamented in death."

Thus gently Betsey phrased her public farewell to the man who had been torn by the hands of the world, and even more torn by his own hands. Their life together had included anguish bordering on madness, long separation, and then mortal sickness. She was thirty years old, handsome, gracious, wealthy (the law had taken care of her inheritance), with only one son, and an elegant country seat. There was every reason to believe that she would remarry.

After she had "departed this life, June 20, 1823, aged forty-seven," "her friends," with "a sense of increasing loss," erected to her a monument. "Left a widow in the prime of life," so the chisel cut into the granite, "she so continued until her death, her affections centering on the memory of her departed HUSBAND."

Acknowledgments

BOSCOBEL RESTORATION, INC., called the Dyckman Papers to my attention and helped my labors along with a grant. My particular gratitude is due to William Barnabas McHenry.

I first set foot in the New-York Historical Society's great library of American history more than forty years ago when I was struggling with my first book, *Doctors on Horseback*. The courtesy and assistance given me now as before by the Society cannot be overstated.

The New York Public Library, of which I am an honorary trustee, is an even older love. I have received the usual invaluable help from the institution that is surely the capital of our great national tradition: self-education.

Among the hills and fields of northwest Connecticut, where I have made my summer home, I have made happy use of the Cornwall Free Library, Hildreth Daniel, Librarian. The offices of the Town Clerk, Kay Fenn, have solaced my neurotic fears of losing manuscript copy with frequent application of a Xerox machine. I am also grateful to the New York Society Library.

In London, I have been assisted by the British Library, the London Library, the Public Record Office, and the National Army Museum. In Edinburgh, I received exemplary help at the West Register House of the Scottish Records Office, J. K. Bates, Director. Mr. and Mrs. Keith Adam, the proprietors of the Wil-

[215]

liam Adam Papers, received my wife and me with charming cordiality.

Professor J. H. Plumb, Master of Christ's College, Cambridge, assisted me on various British matters, waving away my thanks with the charming explanation that we were "fellow members of the republic of letters." Through his recommendation I employed Michael Ryder, then of Trinity College, as a research assistant in British archives.

I am grateful to my wife, Beatrice Hudson Flexner, for thoughtful criticism of my manuscript. George Spater was most informative about William Cobbett, Captain Robert Asprey explained General Dalrymple's activities at the court of Frederick the Great. Frederick W. Stanyer, Executive Director of Boscobel, and Barbara W. Bielenberg, his assistant, have at every turn been both helpful and friendly. Kenneth Wilson has acted as a kindly godfather to the project.

Donald Raiche expertly transcribed, in full or in summary, many hundreds of documents from the Dyckman microfilm. Mrs. Ruth Flaherty typed my manuscript with never-failed cooperation and cheer.

Statement Concerning Sources

THE basic sources for this volume, outweighing by far all others combined, are the Dyckman Papers. The original documents not having been available, I have relied on a complete microfilm at the New-York Historical Society, New York City. There exists a Xerox enlargement of the microfilm running to a total of 3,288 pages. Typed copies or abridgements have been made of the more important documents.

More legible, when the going gets rough, than Xerox sheets, the microfilm reels constitute in the absence of the original papers the fundamental source. They are the touchstone of accuracy for the typescripts. The sequence of exposures in the film cannot, of course, be changed. All other versions have, of necessity, been organized in the same sequence. This dictated solution is far from a happy one, because the microfilm sequence is only partially predictable. Documents from a single year tend to be grouped together, but some have fallen far afield. The last microfilm reel is a grab bag where anything may be found. This situation can only be remedied if the original documents become available for sorting into consistent classification.

Both Boscobel and the New-York Historical Society possess other manuscripts, often important, which cast light on Dyckman's career. Other useful American archives include the Sleepy Hollow Restoration Library, Tarrytown, New York; the Westchester County Clerk's Office and the Westchester County Surrogate's Court, White Plains, New York; and the Westchester Historical Society, Tuckahoe, New York.

In Great Britain and Ireland manuscript sources include: Adam Papers, Blairadam, near Edinburgh, Scotland; British Library, London; National Monuments Record of Scotland, Edinburgh; National Register of Archives, London; Nottingham University Library; Public

Record Office, London; Public Record Office of Ireland, Dublin; Scottish Public Record Office, Edinburgh; Cambridge University Library.

FAMILY BACKGROUND AND CHILDHOOD

The Dyckman manuscripts do not stretch back beyond Dyckman's early manhood, but there are for the earlier years excellent exterior sources. Most important is one of the major monuments of American local history: I. N. Phelps Stokes, *The Iconography of Manhattan Island, 1489–1909*, 6 mammoth volumes, New York, 1925–1928. The 392-page index is extremely difficult to use, but success will quicken like Danae's shower of gold.

Other publications include: Reginald Pelham Bolton, *Washington Heights, Manhattan*, New York, 1936; Cadwallader Colden, *Letters and Papers*, IX, New York, 1937; Thomas H. Edsall, *History of the Town of Kings Bridge*, New York, 1887; Edward Hagaman Hall, *McGown's Pass and Vicinity*, New York, 1905; Sir William Johnson, *Papers*, VII, Albany, 1931; Grenville C. Mackenzie, *Families of the Colonial Town of Philipsburg*, Westport, Connecticut, 1966; *New York Gazette and Weekly Post Boy*, 1/1/1759; *New York Mercury*, 3/8/1756; *Rivington's Gazette*, New York, 9/7/1773, 2/17, 2/24, 1774; James Riker, *Revised History of Harlem*, New York, 1904; William Henry Shelton, *The Jumel Mansion*, Boston, 1916; William A. Tieck, *Riverdale, Kingsbridge, Spuyten Duyvil*, Old Tappan, New York, 1968.

The story of the curse which preceded the father's death comes from a manuscript memorandum by Thomas F. DeVoe, at the New-York Historical Society.

ACTIVITY IN PATRIOT-HELD NEW YORK

Events in the Hudson Valley north of the British lines during the Revolution enter the Dyckman story in various ways: (1) States's adventures from his arrest at Albany to his escape into British-held New York; (2) Dyckman's activities as an employee of the Quartermaster Department in smuggling horses and wagons out of Rebel territory; (3) the tribulations and deeds of Dyckman's mother, brothers, and sisters in Westchester County during the fighting; (4) the difficulties of the grandfather and parents of his future wife during her early years.

The Dyckman Papers cast light on all of these categories except the fourth. Information on all four categories is to be found in published archives: *Calendar of Historical Manuscripts Relating to the War of the Revolution in the Office of the Secretary of State*, ed. E. B. O'Callahan, 2 vols., Albany, 1842; George Clinton, *Papers*, 10 vols., Albany, 1899–1914; *Journals of the Provincial Congress, Provincial Convention, Committee of Safety of New York, 1775–1777*, 3 vols., Albany, 1842; Joel Munsell, *The Annals of Albany*, 10 vols., Albany, 1850–1859; Munsell, *Collections of the History of Albany*, 2 vols., Albany, 1865, 1867; Stokes, *Iconography*. See also: Alexander Clarence Flick, *Loyalism in New York during the American Revolution*, New York, 1901.

LIFE IN BRITISH-HELD NEW YORK

The Dyckman Papers become voluminous during this period. Although he was not considered important enough ever to be mentioned in other sources, many contain valuable insights and information: Carl Leopold Bauermeister, *Revolution in America: Confidential Letters and Journals*, trans. Bernhard A. Uhlendorf, New Brunswick, New Jersey, 1957; Mark Mayo Boatner III, *Encyclopedia of the American Revolution*, New York, 1966; Reginald Pelham Bolton, "The Military Hut-Camp of the War of the Revolution on the Dyckman Farm, Manhattan," *New-York Historical Society Quarterly*, 2 (1918, 1919): 89–97, 130–136; 3 (1919): 15–18; William Dunlap, *A History of the Rise and Progress of the Arts of Design in the United States*, I, New York, 1834; James Thomas Flexner, *The Traitor and the Spy*, Boston, 1953; Thomas Jones, *History of New York During the Revolutionary War*, 2 vols., New York, 1879; Stephen Kemble, *Journals, 1773–1789*, 2 vols., New York, 1883–1884; *Rivington's New York Newspaper: Excerpts from the Loyalist Press, 1773–1783*, New York, 1973; William Smith, *Historical Memoirs*, ed. William H. W. Sabine, 3 vols., New York, 1969–1971; Leslie F. S. Upton, *The Loyal Whig, William Smith at New York and Quebec*, Toronto, 1968; Carl Van Doren, *Benjamin Franklin*, New York, 1938.

QUARTERMASTER ACTIVITIES AND INVESTIGATIONS

The voluminous materials crowding the Dyckman Papers which concern (1) the Department as it functioned in America, and (2) the investigations conducted in New York and London, cannot be discussed separately, since the action of the second category was examining and ruling on the first.

As we have seen, Dyckman assured his clients before his final departure from England that, except for some documents he had given General Dalrymple, "every paper which was in my possession, such as memoranda, remarks, correspondence, etc., etc. . . . are, upon my honor, burnt and destroyed." Whether he did, in fact, destroy anything cannot be determined, but if he did, he could only have pulled out a few conspicuous documents. Paper after surviving paper is highly revealing of matters which the quartermasters would not wish to become public knowledge. The record concerning the dishonest behavior of Erskine, Jr., which Dyckman had specifically threatened to publish, is rehearsed over and over and over again, it sometimes seems *ad infinitum*.

There are spread through the papers many long, detailed, often tabular presentations of presumed quartermaster expenses at various times and places. The majority deal with Dalrymple's tenure, most often with the South Carolina expedition during which Charleston was captured. An extensive digression deals with the building of the sloop *Active* at Rhode Island. These accounts are almost invariably in the hands of professional copyists, which indicates that they were prepared for presentation to investigating boards. Dates of submission are almost never indicated. It is, therefore, impossible to know which of the many revisions these papers represent, or, indeed, whether they are discards never submitted.

Various official rulings are sprinkled through the Dyckman Papers, some significantly annotated with Dyckman's rebuttals. There is almost no personal correspondence with the investigators. Communication seems to have been face-to-face. If letters were written, they were not kept.

Important documents on the investigations, including communications between Dyckman's clients, often discussing his role, are separately filed at the New-York Historical Society. The William Adam papers at Blairadam, near Edinburgh, contain relevant correspondence running to hundreds of letters.

The British Public Record Office has preserved copious records of the various investigations, including Minutes of the Commissioners for Auditing the Public Accounts. These have been exhumed and abstracted for me by Michael Ryder of Trinity College, Cambridge.

Extremely valuable are the *Proceedings of a Board of General Officers of the British Army at New York, 1781*, New York, 1916; *The Seventh Report of the Commissioners Appointed to Examine, Take and State the Public Account of the Kingdom*, [London], 1782.

The bibliography of the Clinton-Cornwallis controversy is much too extended to be rehearsed here. Of particular interest concerning the quartermaster dilemma are: Sir Henry Clinton, *The American Rebellion, Sir Henry Clinton's Narrative of his Campaigns, 1775–1782, with an Appendix of Original Documents*, ed. William B. Willcox, New Haven, 1954; Clinton, *Authentic Copies of Letters between Sir Henry Clinton, K.B., and the Commissioners for Auditing the Public Accounts*, London, 1793 (a copy with Clinton's manuscript notations is in the University Library, Cambridge); Charles C. Cornwallis, *An Answer to that Part of the Narrative of Lieutenant General Sir Henry Clinton, K.B., which relates to the Conduct of Lieutenant General Earl Cornwallis*, London, 1783; William B. Willcox, *Portrait of a General: Sir Henry Clinton in the War of Independence*, New York, 1964.

For a discussion of the role of prerogative in British society see J. H. Plumb, *The Growth of Political Stability in England, 1675–1725*, London, 1969.

THE QUARTERMASTERS

Concerning none of Dyckman's quartermasters have any comprehensive accounts been published. I was forced, as the following list demonstrates, to pick up family and biographical information bit by bit from a wide variety of sources.

The ranks and regiments of every quartermaster may be pursued in the annually published British *Army Lists*.

HENRY BRUEN: *Beetham Abstracts*, VII, Public Record Office of Ireland; *Burke's Irish Family Records*, London, 1976; *Burke's Landed Gentry*, London, 1937; Eugene Devereaux, *Chronicles of the Plumstead Family*, Philadelphia, 1887; *National Library Reports on Private Collections*, No. 20.

LORD CATHCART: *Cambridge History of British Foreign Policy*, I, New York, 1970; G. E. Cockayne, *Complete Peerage*, III, London, 1913; Devereaux, *Plumstead Family; Dictionary of National Biography;* P. R. Drummond, *Perthshire in Bygone Days;* James Thomas Flexner, *America's Old Masters*, New York, 1939; Flexner, *Traitor;* E. Maxtone Graham, *The Beautiful Mrs. Graham and Her Cathcart Circle*, London, 1927.

JOHN DALRYMPLE: Information from Captain Robert Asprey; Stair Manuscripts, Scottish Record Office; James Balfour, *Scottish Peerage*, VII, Edinburgh, 1911; *Cambridge History;* Sir Henry Clinton to the Duke of Newcastle, 3/26/1780, Collection of the Duke of Newcastle; H. H. Dalrymple, *Catalogue of the Pictures at Lockinch Castle*, [n.p.], 1912; John Dalrymple, Fifth Earl (one of many pamphlets by the quartermaster's father), *The State of the Public Debts . . . as they stand on the Fifth of January, 1783. Likewise how they will stand if the War continues, on the Fifth of January, 1784 . . . together with some thoughts on the extent to which the State may be benefited by economy*, London, 1783; John Dalrymple, "Narrative of the Circumstances attending General Dalrymple's taking possession of his Appointment as Quartermaster General in America," ms. at British Library, Add. mss. 33.030 f 452-7; C. H. Dick, *History of the By-Ways of Galloway and Carrick*, London, 1916; *Dictionary of National Biography;* P. H. M'Kerlie, *History of the Lands and Their Owners, Galloway*, Wigtown, 1906; Walter Scott, *The Bride of Lammermoor;* Scott, *Chronicles of Cannongate;* Margaret Stuart and Paul James Balfour, *Scottish Family History*, Edinburgh and London, 1930.

SIR WILLIAM ERSKINE: David Beverage, *Between the Ochils and the Forth*, London and Edinburgh, 1888; Andrew Storer Cunningham, *Culross Past and Present*, Leven, 1910; Cunningham, *Romantic Culross*, Dunfermline, 1902; G. E. Cockayne, *Complete Baronetage*, V, Exeter, 1906; John G. Dunbar, *The Historic Architecture of Scotland*, London, 1966; William Fraser, *Memorials of the Family of Wemyss*, Edinburgh, 1888.

ARCHIBALD ROBERTSON: *Burke's Landed Gentry;* Archibald Robertson, *Diaries and Sketches*, ed. Henry Miller Lydenburg, New York, 1930.

WILLIAM SHERRIFF: The most obscure of the quartermasters, Sherriff eluded my researches in England. His testimony printed in the *Seventh Report*, Appendix 13, gives a short résumé of his career as a quartermaster.

LIFE IN ENGLAND — FIRST PERIOD

Far from home, separated from most of their close human connections, and often not actively employed, Loyalists in England voluminously described in their letters and diaries their ways of life, their reactions to their plights and environments. This wealth of material has only to a very small extent been harvested. Mary Beth Norton's reliable *The British-Americans: The Loyalist Exiles in England, 1774–1789*, Boston, 1972, is a partial exception, but remains primarily concerned with government acts and their effect.

My own concern with the adventures of Americans in London during the Revolution and its aftermath goes back far before my work on Dyckman. I have in a group of books dealt with the American School of Painters in London: *America's Old Masters; John Singleton Copley*, Boston, 1948; *The Light of Distant Skies*, New York, 1954; and *Gilbert Stuart*, New York, 1955. In *The Traitor and the Spy*, I was concerned with Benedict Arnold's tribulations in England after the treason. I shall make no effort to repeat the bibliographies in these volumes.

Since Dyckman was not a significant enough figure to attract documentation from outside, his own papers are, except for a mention in the writings of Peter Van Schaack, the only specific sources for his personal life in London. Happily, the material in the Dyckman Papers is voluminous.

That Dyckman settled within a stone's throw of that famous architectural development, the Adam brothers' Adelphi, made it possible accurately to define his immediate environment. Almost all the buildings have been torn down, but writings on the subject are so copious that only a small selection can be cited: Robert and James Adam, *The Architectural Works*, 3 vols., London, 1778–1782; D. G. C. Allan, *The*

Houses of the Royal Society of Arts, London, 1974; A. T. Bolton, *The Architecture of Robert and James Adam,* 2 vols., London, 1922; John Fleming, *Robert Adam and His Circle,* London, 1962; John Summerton, *Georgian London,* London, 1947; Summerton, *Architecture in Britain,* Baltimore, 1954; Henry Benjamin Wheatley, *The Adelphi and Its Site,* London, 1885.

George Street can still be found although it is not now a cul-de-sac but joined by steps with the Strand.

The light which the Dyckman Papers cast on the situation of the Loyalists who wished to move back to American territory when the war came to an end indicates that the activities of legal bodies in the new United States were much less determining on individual destinies than the history book would have us believe. For a partial discussion see Oscar Zeichner, "The Loyalist Problem in New York after the Revolution," in *New York History,* 21 (1940): 284–302.

Dyckman is mentioned in Henry Cruger Van Schaack, *The Life of Peter Van Schaack, Embracing Selections of his Correspondence and Other Writings during the American Revolution and his Exile in England,* New York, 1842. See also Peter Van Schaack, *Laws of New York from the Year 1691 to 1773 inclusive,* 2 vols., New York, 1774.

BACK IN THE UNITED STATES

The Dyckman Papers, supplemented by other documents at Boscobel, give such full information concerning Dyckman's stay in the Hudson Valley that there is little need for further information. This is fortunate, since the paucity of other sources reflects how private, indeed how obscure, was the retirement that he established for himself. The name of the owner is not even mentioned in the valuable description of King's Grange found in William Strickland, *Journal of a Tour in the United States of America, 1794–1795,* New York, 1950. See also E. Cowles Chorely, *History of St. Philip's Church in the Highlands (Including up to 1840 St. Peter's Church in the Manor of Courtlandt),* New York, 1912; Angus Davidson, *Miss Douglas of New York,* New York, 1953; William J. Kellener, *History of Verplanck,* New York, 1949; Sung Bok Kim, "The Manor of Courtlandt and Its Tenants, 1697–1783," a thesis submitted to Michigan State University, 1966, University Microfilms,

Ann Arbor, Michigan; Henry Onderdonk, *Revolutionary Incidents of Suffolk and King's Counties*, New York, 1849; Emma L. Patterson, *Peekskill in the American Revolution*, Peekskill, New York, 1944; James Thacher, *Military Journal of the American Revolution*, Hartford, 1862; United States, Bureau of the Census, *Heads of Families at the First Census of the United States Taken in the Year 1790*, New York/Washington, 1907–1908. Various volumes cited under the heading "Activity in Patriot-held New York," also contain material concerning this later period.

SECOND LONDON STAY

Most of the sources for this period have already been cited under various overlapping headings.

WILLIAM ADAM: Papers at Blairadam; *Dictionary of National Biography*; John Gibson Lockhart, *Memoirs of the Life of Sir Walter Scott*, many editions.

WILLIAM COBBETT: Information from George Spater; Lewis Saul Benjamin, *Life and Letters of William Cobbett*, 2 vols., London, 1913; G. D. H. Cole, *Life of William Cobbett*, London, 1947; Robert Huish, *Memoirs of the Late William Cobbett*, 2 vols., London, 1836; Lewis Melville, *Life and Letters of William Cobbett*, 2 vols., 1913.

WILLIAM ERSKINE THE YOUNGER: It seems inconceivable that no full account exists of this picturesque and important character, but I was unable to locate any in the British Library, the Royal Army Museum, London, or elsewhere. Most of the publications cited about his father also have bearing on him. See also *Dictionary of National Biography*; *Journal of the Society of Army Historical Research*, 23 (1955): 125–126; Francis Seymour Larpent, *The Private Journal of . . . during the Peninsular War*, London, 1853; Robert Ballard Long, *Peninsular Cavalry*, ed. T. H. McGuffie, London, 1951; William F. P. Napier, *History of the War in the Peninsula and the South of France from 1807 to 1814*, many editions; Henry Smith, Sr., *Autobiography*, ed. G. C. Moore Smith, London, 1903.

LAST YEARS

For this period, the flood of documents in the Dyckman Papers greatly diminishes, undoubtedly a reflection of Dyckman's incapacity through sickness. There are revealing papers concerning the settling of his estate. The inventory will be found at the Westchester County Surrogate's Court, White Plains, New York, File 8-1807.

THE ORIGINAL BOSCOBEL IN ENGLAND: Thomas Blount, *Boscobel or the History of His Sacred Majesty's Most Miraculous Preservation after the Battle of Worcester*, London, 1660; John Byng, *The Torrington Diaries, Containing Tours through England and Wales between the Years 1781 and 1794*, New York, 1936; Edward Clarendon, *The History of the Rebellion and the Civil Wars in England*, III, Part I, Oxford, 1819; Allen Fea, *The Flight of the King*, London, 1908.

STATES DYCKMAN'S BOSCOBEL: Material from the archives of Boscobel Restoration, Inc. Information from William Barnabas McHenry, Frederick W. Stanyer, and Barbara W. Bielenberg of Boscobel.

Index

Adam, James and Robert, 47, 95, 212, 225–226
Adam, William, 100, 101, 158–160, 162–163, 164, 165, 173, 176, 190, 192, 193, 194, 195, 198, 199, 227
Adelphi, the (London), 47–48, 156
Alarm Galley (ship), 50
Albany, N.Y., Dyckman's arrest at, 9, 19–20
Albany Post Road, 113
Alexander, William, 179
Alice's Coffee House (London), 176
Anne, queen of Scotland, 97
Arnold, Benedict, 60, 120
Ashton, William, character in *Bride of Lammermoor*, 96
"Associated Loyalists," 69
Auditors of Imprest, investigation of quartermasters, 52–55, 57–58, 62, 73, 99, 101

Bailie, Dr., 190
Bauermeister, Carl Leopold, 38
Benson, Derrick, 130
biographer, task of, 4, 5
biography, 3–4, 5
Black Horse Tavern, 11, 12. *See also* McGown's Tavern
Blake, Elizabeth Dyckman (sister), 121, 124
Bloomingdale Road, N.Y.C., 11

Board of General Officers of the British Army (1781), 64–68, 185–186, 223
Board of Refugees, 69
Boscobel, Dyckman mansion, 5, 140n, 151, 207–208, 209, 210, 211–213; restored, 5, 210n
Boscobel, Scotland, site of the "Royal Oak," 208–209
Boston, Mass., 25, 32
Boswell, James, 48
Boxley, Mrs., 71
Braddock, Edward, 27, 28
Brandywine, Battle of, 35
Brewer, Eleanor, 31, 64, 131
Brewer, States Dyckman, 31, 64, 131, 135, 183, 206–207
Bride of Lammermoor (Scott), 96
Britain: aristocratic society in, 7, 45–47, 48–49, 133; attitude toward Revolution, 22, 32, 58; Loyalists in, 44–45, 80–81, 84–85; reaction to French Revolution, 177–178; taxation in, 7, 58
British aristocracy, financial prerogatives, 7, 48–49, 77–78, 160, 171, 184, 190, 196–197
British army: in New York City, 24, 26, 69; profiteering by quartermasters (*see* Quartermaster Department, British army); treatment of colonists, 24, 69

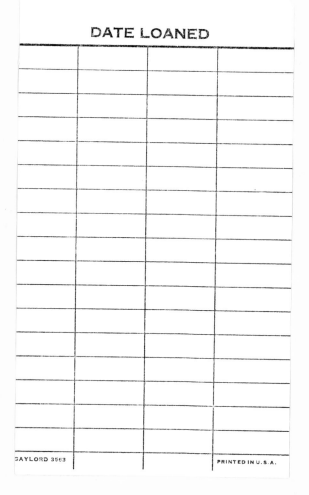

DATE LOANED

GAYLORD 3563

PRINTED IN U.S.A.